# CHUANG TSU
## INNER CHAPTERS

PHOTOGRAPHY BY JANE ENGLISH
CALLIGRAPHY BY GIA-FU FENG

# CHUANG TSU
## INNER CHAPTERS

A COMPANION VOLUME TO *Tao Te Ching*

TRANSLATED BY GIA-FU FENG AND JANE ENGLISH

UPDATED TRANSLATION WITH OVER 100 NEW PHOTOGRAPHS

INTRODUCTION BY CHUNGLIANG AL HUANG

HAY HOUSE, INC.

Carlsbad, California · New York City · London · Sydney
Johannesburg · Vancouver · Hong Kong · New Delhi

Originally published in 1974 in hardcover by Alfred A. Knopf, Inc., and in softcover by Vintage Books.

Knopf/Vintage 1st edition copyright ©1974 by Jane English and Gia-fu Feng ISBN 0-394-71990-5

Earth Heart 2nd edition copyright ©1997 by Jane English and Carol Wilson ISBN 0-934747-16-4

Amber Lotus Publishing 3rd edition copyright ©2000 by Jane English and Carol Wilson ISBN 978-1-56937-282-1

Amber Lotus Publishing 4th edition copyright ©2008 by Jane English and Carol Wilson ISBN 978-1-60237-117-0

Copyright © 2014 by Jane English and Carol Wilson

Published and distributed in the United States by: Hay House, Inc.: www.hayhouse.com® • Published and distributed in Australia by: Hay House Australia Pty. Ltd.: www.hayhouse.com.au • Published and distributed in the United Kingdom by: Hay House UK, Ltd.: www.hayhouse.co.uk • Published and distributed in the Republic of South Africa by: Hay House SA (Pty), Ltd.: www .hayhouse.co.za • Distributed in Canada by: Raincoast Books: www.raincoast.com • Published in India by: Hay House Publishers India: www.hayhouse.co.in

Library of Congress Control Number: 2014946658

Tradepaper ISBN: 978-1-4019-4659-3

10  9  8  7  6  5  4  3  2  1
1st Hay House edition, November 2014

Printed in the United States of America

*Chuang Tsu: Inner Chapters* is a companion volume to Gia-fu Feng and Jane English's translation of Lao Tsu's *Tao Te Ching*, which has enjoyed great success since its publication in 1972.

Very little is known about Chuang Tsu, and that little is inextricably woven into legend. It is said that he was a contemporary of the Confucian philosopher Mencius, who was an official in the Lacquer Garden of Meng in Honan Province around the 4th century B.C. Chuang Tsu was to Lao Tsu as Saint Paul was to Jesus and Plato to Socrates. He was a captivating philosopher who expanded Lao Tsu's teachings.

While the other philosophers were busying themselves with the practical matters of government and rules of conduct, Chuang Tsu transcended the *whang cheng*, the illusory dust of the world—thus anticipating Zen Buddhism's emphasis on a state of emptiness or ego transcendence. With humor, imagery, and fantasy, he captures the depth of Chinese thinking. The seven "Inner Chapters" presented in this translation are accepted by scholars as being definitely the work of Chuang Tsu. Another twenty-six chapters are of questionable origin; they are interpretations of his teaching and may have been added by later commentators.

This is an updated version of the translation of *Chuang Tsu: Inner Chapters* that was originally published in 1974. Like the original Chinese, this version uses gender-neutral language wherever possible. This edition includes many new photographs by Jane English and an introduction by Tai Ji master Chungliang Al Huang, who has been highly successful in bringing to the West the wisdom of the East by teaching Tai Ji, calligraphy, and the Chinese classics through his Living Tao Foundation.

# FOREWORD TO THE 2014 EDITION

The first book I did with Gia-fu Feng, the *Tao Te Ching*, was published in 1972. The next year we began a book on the writings of Chuang Tsu. We approached Chuang Tsu the same way we did the *Tao Te Ching*, by working with the translations at group meetings at our big communal house in Colorado. Although Chuang Tsu is quite humorous, we treated it very seriously, resulting in lively debates over the meanings behind the stories.

One of the things I personally like about Chuang Tsu's work, compared to the *Tao Te Ching*, is that it is not as "pure." While the *Tao Te Ching* seems almost unreachable, Chuang Tsu's *Inner Chapters* are about imperfections. In chapter five particularly, we are confronted by a parade of physically imperfect characters: a cripple, a hunchback, and a man with no toes. "Can the mind be perfect," asks Chuang Tsu, "while the body is deformed?" I recognize imperfections in myself, and this is part of what appeals to me about Chuang Tsu's *Inner Chapters.*

I never studied art, but I spent my early years out in the woods looking at nature. I drank it in and I saw the balance, the harmony, the movement, and how it all fit together. Even before I met Gia-fu, I imagined my photographs as Chinese landscape paintings. I especially liked creating photographs that teetered on the boundary between being and nonbeing—tree branches that delicately merge with the sky, fog almost obscuring a mountain, details of shells or grass that are almost unrecognizable. This was a way to go beyond the too-static "thingness" of ordinary consciousness, a doorway to a vastness that seemed to be my native land. Through my imagery I was intuitively going around and beyond words and seeing the ineffable, sometimes called *Tao*, through nature.

Over the years I have gradually come to realize that the living Tao cannot be photographed any more than it can be described. Yet both words and images can point toward Tao, can be "fingers pointing to the moon." A Zen teaching story tells of the importance of not mistaking the finger that points to the moon for the moon itself, of not mistaking the guide for the goal. Words and images can be delightful "fingers," guides along the way.

Is *Tao* simply a word we use to point beyond words, and to fill in where the structure of language demands a subject, even when, in the unnameable oneness, there is no subject or object of which to speak?

As we are born, we fall away from a oneness that is beyond light, but which is often spoken of as light. I was unconsciously reaching back for that light in much of my photography work. I was mistaking the outer world light for the inner light. Often there has been a feeling of sadness or longing in my photographing. I was looking for something that was separate from me rather than knowing Tao that is everywhere.

For many years, photographing was for me an unconscious attempt to heal myself. Photographing allowed me to play in nature as I had as a child. Holding a camera took care of the need to be doing something and allowed the rest of me to just be present, in the Tao.

The pairing of calligraphy and photographs with the text does an end run around our Western logical minds. It keeps our interest, even when our logical minds are befuddled. Perhaps the confusion we Westerners sometimes feel while reading Chuang Tsu comes from certain standards and assumptions we make—that there ought to be a linear, logical way of understanding it. But with Chuang Tsu, linearity is simply not

there. The reader assumes the writing is linear, then wonders whether there is something wrong with his or her own understanding. Chuang Tsu just doesn't make linear sense.

But now, 40 years after our translation of Chuang Tsu's *Inner Chapters* was first published, people may be ready for it. It is becoming more and more obvious in our world that some of the rational, linear ways of approaching things don't always work. People are becoming more open to alternatives. Perhaps they are beginning to see that many of the solutions to the difficulties arising today may not be mechanical or scientific solutions, or even political solutions, but spiritual solutions. It's all about how we see ourselves and our reality. Chuang Tsu can help us with this.

I invite you to enter into this book with a spirit of adventure, mindful of the paradox of using words and images to approach the ineffable Tao. Explore with me this treasure that has come from the East into our Western world.

—*Jane English*

# INTRODUCTION

## BY CHUNGLIANG AL HUANG

I bow to Lao Tsu, and humbly submit to the philosophy of a simple, natural world harmony of the ineffable Tao. And I vow to study his perennial wisdom, and forever follow the Way prescribed in the crystalline classic of the *Tao Te Ching*.

But I love and cherish Chuang Tsu. I admire his penetrating insight, acerbic wit, no-nonsense clarity, and his "flesh and blood" humanity. And I treasure his wealth of delightful, thought-provoking anecdotes and parables, his original mind, and his "windflow" personality.

And most of all, I adore his humor and laughter. He is my hero and my kindred soul.

As a child in China, my first encounter with Chuang Tsu was in a popular Chinese cinema. Chuang Tsu was a magician who dreamt and transformed himself into a butterfly. In the same movie, Chuang Tsu and his wife passed by a cemetery and observed a woman fanning furiously at the grave of her newly deceased husband. Upon inquiring sympathetically, they were shocked to hear the widow's motive: "I promised my husband that I would not remarry until the earth on his grave was completely dry!"

To test his wife's devotion and his own lack of faith, Chuang Tsu contrived a fake death and invented a melodrama of desire, betrayal, and the inconsistency of the human heart. It was quite a dynamic show, climaxing with Chuang Tsu's widow desperately chopping open his coffin to find him resurrected and laughing with delight . . .

The story was the invention of the theater, taking great liberty rehashing the many colorful folktales of and by Chuang Tsu. But I was captivated. I became an undying devotee of Chuang Tsu and found myself diligently absorbed in his writings, which otherwise would have been intimidating and incomprehensible to my immature mind. Instead, I found an easy entry into the treasures of his genius, and have continued to enjoy and marvel at his endless wealth of resourcefulness.

For most Chinese, Chuang Tsu represents the best of what we admire in a person. He is brilliant and mystical, philosophically pragmatic, witty and delightful, successful in being untainted by the need to succeed, and, most important, he is free. He is his own person, wandering through life like wind and water, enjoying its many delights without cumbersome attachments. The core of Chuang Tsu is this sense of ultimate freedom. He manages to exist quite sanely in the chaotic world, enjoying the best of humanity, without being dragged under. He seems to see through all the veils of human sufferings camouflaging the eternal truth.

Chuang Tsu's greatest contribution to the perennial wisdom of Taoism was his ability to expound further and deeper on Lao Tsu's simple maxims, yet use terms clear to everyman. While the Old

Master succinctly, in 5,000 words, gave the world the essential philosophy in the *Tao Te Ching*, Chuang Tsu expanded it into a sophisticated and joyful personal freedom.

Chuang Tsu was a man of this world, totally in touch with the politics and the social discontent of his time. Unlike the seemingly illusive and enigmatic Lao Tsu, Chuang Tsu was a real person with true emotions and feelings.[1] With a keen appreciation of the relativity of the things of the world and a profound sense of human nature in all its complexities, he sought to understand, accept, and resolve these contradictions and foibles. His idea of an enlightened person is one who transcends wishes and fears, and is eventually completely free.

Although most of his writings are serious and rigorous in developing the Taoist themes, he is distinguished by his creative and imaginative mind. Chuang Tsu can be uncompromisingly honest and incisive when he comes to social commentary on human inconsistencies and frailties. He spares no one and nothing. He intends to sting and wake the readers into becoming fully human, and endeavors to penetrate their delusions, to come through with a simpler truth. Humor is his forte, his net and cushion to catch and comfort his slightly stunned reader's sudden enlightenment.

As a philosopher he is deep, yet fathomable. As a teacher he reaches the depth of the human heart; he cajoles and enthralls. As a writer he is considered one of the greatest prose masters of Chinese literature. His classic style is lean and sleek, unencumbered and right to the potent points. His brilliance is in his free-flowing association of ideas, profoundly deep in thought, yet light, witty, and accessible. Foremost, Chuang Tsu represents the creative and original mind. And he is unique and special for being one of the very few philosophers who laughed.

The first of the seven Inner Chapters is entitled *Xiao Yao Yu*—translated here as "Happy Wandering." But the intrinsic meaning is in the images of the Chinese symbols. *Xiao* depicts a person letting go of unnecessary burdens of worldly and egoistic encumbrances. *Yao* suggests a place of the immortals transcending the tainted and polluted earthly realm. *Yu* creates a vision of the simple joy of fishes in water. All three Chinese symbols visually float and sail, balancing on the brushstroke of the flowing movement of nature—*The Watercourse Way!*

It is with this deep longing for transcendence that Chuang Tsu begins to explore and weave the threads of his Taoist tapestry. He tells stories to enrich our imagination and stimulate our senses, and pumps deep into our subconscious to help us get in touch with our deepest and innermost potentialities. He wishes to set us free.

In the second chapter, *Qi Wu Luen*, "The Equality of All Things," Chuang Tsu eloquently discusses ecology with the key concept of "Heaven and Earth and I are co-created; the ten-thousand-things and I are one." He concludes with the famous "butterfly dream." Chuang Tsu dreamt of being a butterfly. And while he was in the dream, he felt he could flutter his wings and flitter here and there, totally being as real as a butterfly. But upon waking up, he realized that he was really Chuang Tsu. He then pondered whether he was actually Chuang Tsu dreaming of being a butterfly, or a butterfly dreaming of being Chuang Tsu. This powerful inner dialogue suggests that perhaps life is indeed a dream, that all human beings are merely on a journey, floating down the eternal river of time.

In *Yang Shen Zu,* "The Secret of Growth" or the preservation of a healthful life, Chuang Tsu gives us the best example of the Taoist concept of *Wu Wei,* the power of noninterference. Cook Ding, who cuts his oxen with a knife that finds no resistance, is the supreme and ultimate Tao master for all to emulate. Also in this chapter, we marvel at the unlimitedness of knowledge and wisdom, and learn to submit to the art of not overextending in order to preserve energy and life-force in our limited human life. We also learn to transcend the fear and regrets of this ephemeral existence. Chuang Tsu reassures us that the Fire of Life in our spirit is eternal.

*Ren Jian Sse* contains the teachings of Chuang Tsu on "Human Affairs." *Ren* is everything human; *Jian* is the light that shines through when one knocks at the door, only to find it open; *Sse* is the earthly world we live in. In this chapter we have a pithy discussion about

meditation, "the fasting" of the mind/heart, and about the way of cultivating the vital essence of Ch'i (Qi). He also gives us a perfect example of the usefulness of uselessness.

In *Te Chun Fu,* "Signs of Full Virtue," Chuang Tsu emphasizes the cultivation of inner virtue, in lieu of the relentless struggle for external and superficial achievements of human vanity.

In *Da Zhong Sse,* "The Great Master," Chuang Tsu describes the "true person," also the "arrived person" and the "spiritual person." He speaks about being at peace and rejoicing in fate and destiny.

Finally in *Yin Di Wang,* "The Sage King," Chuang Tsu expounds on the wisdom of "no mind" or "mirror mind" of the "perfect human" who seeks no fame, makes no plans, escapes the burden of overactivity and the slavery of superficial knowledge, who experiences the infinite and wanders where there is no path. This sagely person is graciously receptive to all that nature bestows, is unselfconscious, and practices the art of emptiness. With the mirror's pure reflection, this cultivated being grasps nothing, expects nothing; reflects without prejudice, succeeds without effort.

This chapter ends with the tragic story of interference, warning the world to leave well enough alone. As universally acknowledged, the road to hell is often paved with best intentions; the sure way to deviate from Tao is overindulgence and overstepping our bounds to compete and interfere with Great Mother Nature.

Taoism is neither a religion nor a specific school of thought in China. It reflects the fundamental character of Chinese thinking, a deeply rooted attitude toward life, family, society, and the world. It is about the rhythm of life, developed for human use in daily living. Chuang Tsu combines the metaphysical and the pragmatic philosophies into palatable maxims for everyone who is interested in self-cultivation and in delving deeper into personal exploration.

While Confucianism provides an overall structure to attain social order, Chuang Tsu's freewheeling Taoist explorations provide us creative, safe releases from the confines and restraints of trying mindlessly to be good and proper. Although it often seems that Chuang Tsu ridicules Confucian ethics as superficial rigidity, he merely uses the extremes to drive home a point. He is the master of paradox and relativity. As a supreme storyteller, he liberally exaggerates, sets free wild and imaginary fantasies, and trusts that we, the readers, can keep up with his wit and romantic adventures. Just as we freely allow the humorists to be outrageous and profound at the same time, Chuang Tsu must be read and enjoyed with the same freedom.

I suggest reading Chuang Tsu with children to gain further insights into these fantastic fables and anecdotes. At the very least, be "childlike" at heart when you read these pages. Avoid the sin of concretization of ideas and trapping yourself with linear thoughts. Invite in the gigantic "thousand li" fish Kun who transforms to the big bird Peng to meet General Clouds and Great Nebulous, and let the small fishes converse with the Spirit of River and Ocean; and listen in when Chuang Tsu speaks to the skull[2] about the meaning of life and death. In Chuang Tsu's "Wonderland," Lewis Carroll's unicorn and Alice are frequent visitors!

Finally, Chuang Tsu helps us to take all serious matters lightly, and encourages us to be the "Laughing Philosopher."

Enjoy!

*Chungliang Al Huang* is an internationally respected Tai Ji master and authority on East/West cultural synthesis. He is the author of the classic *Embrace Tiger, Return to Mountain,* and of *Quantum Soup*; and coauthor with Alan Watts of *Tao: The Watercourse Way,* and with Jerry Lynch of *Thinking Body, Dancing Mind* and *Mentoring: The Tao of Giving and Receiving Wisdom.* The website for his Living Tao Foundation is www.livingtao.org.

# CHUANG TSU
## INNER CHAPTERS

# CONTENTS

Chapter 1  Happy Wandering  1

Chapter 2  The Equality of All Things  17

Chapter 3  The Secret of Growth  49

Chapter 4  Human Affairs  59

Chapter 5  Signs of Full Virtue  89

Chapter 6  The Great Master  109

Chapter 7  The Sage King  143

逍遙游

CHAPTER ONE

# HAPPY WANDERING

北冥有魚其名為鯤鯤之大不知其幾千里也
化而為鳥其名為鵬鵬之背不知其幾千里也怒而
飛其翼若垂天之雲是鳥也海運則將徙於南冥
南冥者天池也齊諧者志怪者也諧之言曰鵬之
徙於南冥也水擊三千里摶扶搖而上者九萬里
去以六月息者也野馬也塵埃也生物之以息相吹也
天之蒼蒼其正色邪其遠而無所至極邪其視下也亦若是則已矣且夫水之積也不厚
則其負大舟也無力覆杯水於坳堂之上則芥為之舟
置杯焉則膠水淺而舟大也風之積也不厚則其負大翼也無力
故九萬里則風斯在下矣而後乃今培風背負青天而莫之夭閼者而後乃今將圖南

In the Northern Ocean there is a fish called Kun which is many thousand li[3] in size. It changes into a bird named Peng whose back is many thousand li in breadth. When it rises and flies, its wings are like clouds filling the sky.

When this bird moves across the ocean, it heads for the South Sea, the Celestial Lake. In Chi Hsieh's record of wonders it says: "When Peng is heading toward the Southern Ocean it splashes along the water for three thousand li. It rises with the wind and wings its way up to ninety thousand li; it flies for six months, and then it rests." Heat shimmers in the air like galloping horses, dust floats like the morning mist, and living creatures are blown about in the sky.

The sky is blue. Is that really so? Or does it only look blue because it stretches off into infinity? When Peng looks down from above, it will also seem blue. A large boat draws a great deal of water. Pour a cup of water into a hollow in the ground, and a mustard seed can float there like a little ship. Place the cup in it, and it will not move, because the water is shallow and the boat is large. Only at a certain height is there enough air space for a great wingspan. So Peng rises to ninety thousand li, and there is enough air below him. Then he mounts the wind, and with the blue sky at his back, and nothing in his way, he heads for the south.

A cicada and a young dove laugh at Peng, saying, "When we try hard we can reach the trees, but sometimes we fall short and drop on the ground. How is it possible to rise ninety thousand li and head south?" If you go into the country, you take enough food for three meals and come back with your stomach as full as ever. If you travel a hundred li, you grind enough grain for an overnight stay. If you travel a thousand li, you must have three months' supply.

What do these two small creatures know? Little knowledge is not to be compared with great knowledge, nor a short life with a long life.

How do we know this is so?

The morning mushroom knows nothing of twilight and dawn, nor the chrysalis of spring and autumn. These are the short-lived. South of Chu there is a ming-ling tree whose spring is five hundred years and autumn five hundred years. A long time ago there was a tortoise whose spring was eight thousand years and autumn eight thousand years. Peng Chu is a man famous for his long life. Isn't it sad that everyone wants to imitate him?

蜩與學鳩笑之曰我決起而飛槍榆枋時則不至而控於地而已矣
奚以之九萬里而南為莽蒼者三飡而反腹猶果然適百里者宿舂糧
適千里者三月聚糧之二蟲又何知小知不及大知小年不及大年奚以知其然也
朝菌不知晦朔蟪蛄不知春秋此小年也楚之南有冥靈者以五百歲為春五百歲為秋
古有大椿者以八千歲為春八千歲為秋而彭祖乃今以久特聞眾人匹之不亦悲乎

湯之問棘也是已窮髮之北有冥海者天池也有魚焉其廣數十里未有知其脩者其名為鯤有鳥焉其名為鵬背若泰山翼若垂天之雲摶扶搖羊角而上者九萬里絕雲氣負青天然後圖南且適南冥也斥鴳笑之曰彼且奚適也我騰躍而上不過數仞而下翱翔蓬蒿之間此亦飛之至也而彼且奚適也此小大之辯也故夫知效一官行比一鄉德合一君而徵一國者其自視也亦若此矣而宋榮子猶然笑之且舉世而譽之而不加勸舉世而非之而不加沮定乎內外之分辯乎榮辱之境斯已矣彼其於世未數數然也雖然猶有未樹也夫列子御風而行泠然善也旬有五日而後反彼於致福者未數數然也此雖免乎行猶有所待者也若夫乘天地之正而御六氣之辯以遊無窮者彼且惡乎待哉故曰至人無己神人無功聖人無名

In the dialogue of Tang and Chi there is the same story: "In the barren north there is a dark sea, the Celestial Lake. There is a fish living there several thousand li in breadth and no one knows its length. Its name is Kun. And there too lives a bird called Peng. Its back is like Mount Tai and its wings are like clouds across the heavens. It spirals up to ninety thousand li, beyond the clouds and the wind, and with blue sky above it heads south to the South Sea. A quail by the marsh laughs, saying, 'Where does he think he is going? I bob up and down a few feet, fluttering among the weeds and bushes. This is perfection in flying. What is he up to?'

"This is the difference between small and great."

Thus, those who are wise enough to hold an official position, fair enough to keep the peace in a community, virtuous enough to be a ruler and govern a state, look upon themselves in the same way.

Yet Sung Yung Tsu laughs at them. For if the whole world praised him, he would not be moved. If the whole world blamed him, he would not be discouraged. He knows the difference between that which is within and that which is without. He is clear about honor and disgrace. But that is all. Though such a person is rare in the world, he is still imperfect.

Lieh Tsu rode on the wind, light and at ease, and returned after fifteen days. Ones as happy as he are rare. Though he no longer needed to walk, he still depended on something. But suppose someone rides on the flow of heaven and earth and the transformation of the six elements and wanders in the infinite. On what is he dependent?

Therefore it is said, "The perfect person has no self, the holy one has no merit, the wise have no reputation."

Yao thought he would cede the empire to Hsu Yu, saying, "When the sun and moon are shining, isn't it hard to see a torch? When the rainy season starts, isn't it a waste of labor to continue to water the fields? If you take over, the empire will be well ruled. I am now the ruler, and I feel inadequate. May I give the empire into your care?"

Hsu Yu said, "You are ruling the empire, and the world is already at peace. If I took your place, I would be doing it for the name. Name is only the shadow of reality. Do I want to be just a shadow? The sparrow building its nest in the deep wood occupies but a single twig. The muskrat drinks only enough from the river to fill its belly. Go in peace, my lord. I have no use for the empire. If the cook at a ritual ceremony is not attending to the food offerings, the priests and the representatives of the dead do not leap over the wine and the meat to take his place."

堯讓天下於許由曰日月出矣而爝火不息其於光也不亦難乎時雨降矣而猶浸灌其於澤也勞乎夫子立而天下治而我猶尸之吾自視缺然請致天下許由曰子治天下天下既已治也而我猶代子吾將為名乎名者實之賓也吾將為賓乎鷦鷯巢於深林不過一枝偃鼠飲河不過滿腹歸休乎君予無所用天下為庖人雖不治庖尸祝不越樽俎而代之矣

Chien Wu questioned Lien Shu: "I heard Chieh Yu telling strange stories, long and fantastic, going on and on without end. I was amazed at his words. They seemed to be as boundless as the Milky Way and had no connection with the way things really are."

Lien Shu asked, "What did he say?"

"Far away on Mount Ku lives a holy man. His flesh and skin are like ice and snow; he is as gentle as a young girl. He eats none of the five grains, but takes deep draughts of the wind and drinks the dew. He rides on clouds and mounts a flying dragon and wanders beyond the four seas.[4] By using his spiritual powers he can protect creatures from sickness and decay, and ensure a rich harvest. I think this is ridiculous and do not believe it."

Lien Shu said, "So it is. The blind cannot appreciate beautiful patterns, the deaf cannot hear the sounds of bells and drums. Blindness and deafness are not just physical; they can be mental too. Yours is a case in point. That holy man with all his virtues looks on all the confusion of the ten thousand things as one. Because of his very existence, the world is emerging from chaos. Why should he do anything about it? Nothing can harm him. A great flood reaching the sky could not drown him. Though a great drought caused metals and rocks to melt and scorched the earth and hills, he would feel no heat. From his own substance he can create philosopher kings like Yao or Shun. Why should he bother with worldly things?"

肩吾問於連叔曰吾聞言於接輿大而無當往而不返吾驚怖其言猶河漢而無極也大有逕庭不近人情焉連叔曰其言謂何哉曰藐姑射之山有神人居焉肌膚若冰雪綽約若處子不食五穀吸風飲露乘雲氣御飛龍而遊乎四海之外其神凝使物不疵癘而年穀熟吾以是狂而不信也連叔曰然瞽者無以與乎文章之觀聾者無以與乎鐘鼓之聲豈唯形骸有聾盲哉夫知亦有之是其言也猶時女也之人也之德也將旁礴萬物以為一世蘄乎亂孰弊弊焉以天下為事之人也物莫之傷大浸稽天而不溺大旱金石流土山焦而不熱是其塵垢粃糠將猶陶鑄堯舜者也孰肯以物為事

宋人資章甫適諸越越人斷髮文身無所用之

堯治天下之民平海內之政往見四子藐姑射之山

汾水之陽窅然喪其天下焉

A person from the state of Sung selling ceremonial caps made a trip to the state of Yueh. But Yueh people, having short hair and tattooed bodies, had no use for them. Yao brought order to the people of the world and ruled wisely over the lands bounded by the four seas. But returning south of the Fen River after his visit to the four sages on Mount Kui, he lost his interest in the empire.

Hui Tsu said to Chuang Tsu, "The King of Wei gave me some seeds from a huge gourd. I planted them and they bore a fruit big enough to hold five bushels. I used it to carry water, but it was too heavy to lift. So I cut it in half to make ladles, but they were too shallow to hold anything. They were big, unwieldy, and useless so I smashed them into pieces."

Chuang Tsu said, "My friend, you are not very intelligent in your use of large things. There was a man from Sung who could make a good salve for chapped hands. His family had had a silk-bleaching business for generations. A traveler heard of this and offered to buy the secret formula for one hundred pieces of gold. The family gathered together to have a conference and said, 'We have been bleaching silk for generations and have earned only a few pieces of gold. Now in one day we can sell the secret for one hundred pieces of gold. Let him have it.'

"The traveler took it and offered it to the King of Wu. Wu and Yueh were at war. The King of Wu entrusted the traveler with the command of his fleet. In the winter the fleet fought a naval battle against Yueh and totally defeated it. The traveler was rewarded with a fief and title.

"In both cases, the cure for chapped hands was the same but was used differently. One man got a title, while the others are still bleaching silk. Now, you had a gourd big enough to hold five bushels. Why didn't you think of making it into a great barrel and using it to float along the rivers and lakes instead of worrying about its being useless for holding anything? Your mind, my friend, is still very cluttered with trivia."

Hui Tsu said, "I have a big ailanthus tree. Its trunk is so gnarled and full of knots that it is impossible to measure it accurately. Its branches are too twisted and crooked for anyone to measure with a compass and square. It stands at the side of the road, but no carpenter would give it a second glance. Now, your words are as big and useless; no one wants to hear what you have to say."

Chuang Tsu replied, "Have you ever watched a wildcat or a weasel? It crouches close to the ground and waits for its prey. Then it leaps up and down, first one way, then the other, until it catches and kills its prey. Then again there is the yak, as great as a cloud shadowing the sky. Big as it is, it cannot catch a mouse. Now, you have this giant tree and are concerned that it is useless. Why don't you plant it on land where nothing grows, in a wild, barren place? There you may saunter idly around it, doing nothing, and lie down to sleep beneath its boughs. No one will try to cut it down. Nothing can harm it since it has no use. How can it cause you any anxiety?"

齊物論

CHAPTER TWO

# THE EQUALITY OF ALL THINGS

Nan Kuo Tsu Chi sat leaning on a low table, gazing at the heavens and sighing; he appeared to be in a trance. His disciple Yen Cheng Tsu Yu, who was standing beside him, exclaimed, "What is this? Can you really make your body like dry wood and your mind like dead ashes? The man leaning on the table is not the one who was here a moment ago."

Tsu Chi said, "Yen, it is good that you asked that. Just now I lost myself. Do you understand? Perhaps you have heard the music of the people but not the music of earth. You may have heard the music of earth but not the music of heaven."

Tsu Yu said, "May I ask you to say more about this?"

Tsu Chi answered, "The universe has a cosmic breath. Its name is wind. Sometimes it is not active; but when it is, angry howls rise from ten thousand openings. Have you ever heard a roaring gale?

"In the mountain forest, deep and fearsome, there are huge trees a hundred arm spans around, with gaps and hollows like nostrils, mouths, and ears, like gouges, goblets, and mortars, and like muddy pools and dirty puddles. The sounds rush out like water, whistle like arrows, scold, suck, shout, wail, moan, and howl. The leading notes are hissing sounds followed by a roaring chorus. Gentle breezes make a small harmony, fierce winds a great one. When the violent gusts subside, all the hollows become quiet. Have you ever seen the shaking and trembling of branches and leaves?"

Tsu Yu said, "The earth's music is the sound from those hollows. The people's music comes from the hollow reed. May I ask about the music of heaven?"

Tsu Chi said, "When the wind blows through the ten thousand different hollows, they all make their own sounds. Why should there be anything else that causes the sound?"

南郭子綦隱机而坐仰天而噓
荅焉似喪其耦顏成子游立侍乎前曰
何居乎形固可使如槁木
而心固可使如死灰乎今之隱机者
非昔之隱机者也子綦曰偃
不亦善乎而問之也今者吾喪我汝知之乎
女聞人籟而未聞地籟女聞地籟而未聞天籟夫
子游曰敢問其方子綦曰夫大塊噫氣
其名為風是唯无作作則萬竅怒呺
而獨不聞之翏翏乎山林之畏佳
大木百圍之竅穴似鼻似口似耳似枅似圈似臼
似洼者似污者激者謞者叱者吸者叫者譹者
宎者咬者前者唱于而隨者唱喁
泠風則小和飄風則大和
厲風濟則眾竅為虛
而獨不見之調調之刁刁乎子游曰地籟則眾竅是已人籟則比竹是已
敢問天籟子綦曰夫吹萬不同而使其自已也咸其自取怒者其誰邪

Great knowledge is all-encompassing; small knowledge is limited. Great words are inspiring; small words are chatter. When we are asleep, we are in touch with our souls. When we are awake, our senses open. We get involved with our activities, and our minds are distracted. Sometimes we are hesitant, sometimes underhanded, and sometimes secretive. Little fears cause anxiety, and great fears cause panic. Our words fly off like arrows, as though we knew what was right and wrong. We cling to our own point of view, as though everything depended on it. And yet our opinions have no permanence; like autumn and winter, they gradually pass away. We are caught in the current and cannot return. We are tied up in knots like an old clogged drain; we are getting closer to death with no way to regain our youth. Joy and anger, sorrow and happiness, hope and fear, indecision and strength, humility and willfulness, enthusiasm and insolence, like music sounding from an empty reed or mushrooms rising from the warm, dark earth, continually appear before us day and night. No one knows whence they come. Don't worry about it! Let them be! How can we understand it all in one day?

If there is no other, there is no I. If there is no I, there is no one to perceive. This is close to the truth, but we do not know why. There must be some primal force, but we cannot discover any proof. I believe it acts, but I cannot see it. I can feel it, but it has no form.

The hundred joints, nine openings, and six organs[5] all function together. Which part do you prefer? Do you like them all equally, or do you have a favorite? Are they not all servants? Can they keep order among themselves, or do they take turns being masters and servants?

It may be that there is indeed a true master. Whether I really feel his existence or not has nothing to do with the way it is.

Once one is given a body it works naturally as long as it lasts. It carries on through hardship and ease and, like a galloping horse, nothing can stop it. Isn't it sad? All through life one toils and sweats, never seeing any result. Weary and exhausted, man has no place to rest his bones. Isn't this a pity? One may say, "There is no death." What good does that do? When the body decays, so does the mind. Is this not a great sorrow? Is life really this absurd? Am I the only one who sees the absurdity? Don't others see it too?

夫随天感心而师之说独旦要师乎
学心无化心心且水本有之无乎无有与
夫心未心无有生无无云之而通而若云乎
生以无有无有无有无有神焉
旦旦解无无独旦本有部
夫无心吹也之无百一云游云去特未定也
果有无无无无无无云无无无有无师
无以无无子识无无无无无无天无辩乎
道无无未信无无无无无无
六无无信无无有无似
道无无无无无无无无无无无死
均有偶墨之無無以无云无无生无无无无死
无无不无死

If one is true to one's self and follows its teaching, who need be without a teacher? Not only those who are experienced and wise may have a teacher; the fools have theirs too. When those who are not true to themselves try to choose between right and wrong, it is as if they set off for Yueh today and arrived yesterday. That would be making what does not exist, exist. How do you make what does not exist, exist? Even the holy man Yu did not know how to do this, much less a person like me.

Words are not just blown air. They have a meaning. If you are not sure what you are talking about, are you saying anything, or are you saying nothing? Words seem different from the chirping of birds. Is there a difference, or isn't

there? How can Tao be so obscure and yet admit of truth and falsehood? How can words be so obscure and yet admit of right and wrong? How can Tao cease to exist? How can words not be heard?

Tao is hidden by partial understanding. The meaning of words is hidden by flowery rhetoric. This is what causes the dissension between the Confucians and the Mohists.[6] What one says is wrong, the other says is right; and what one says is right, the other says is wrong. If the one is right while the other is wrong, and the other is right while the one is wrong, then the best thing to do is to look beyond right and wrong.

物無非彼，物無非是。自彼則不見，自知則知之。故曰彼出於是，是亦因彼。彼是方生之說也。雖然，方生方死，方死方生；方可方不可，方不可方可；因是因非，因非因是。是以聖人不由，而照之於天，亦因是也。是亦彼也，彼亦是也。彼亦一是非，此亦一是非。果且有彼是乎哉？果且無彼是乎哉？彼是莫得其偶，謂之道樞。樞始得其環中，以應無窮。是亦一無窮，非亦一無窮也。故曰莫若以明。

Every thing can be a "that"; every thing can
be a "this." One person cannot see things
as another sees them. You can only know
things through knowing yourself. Therefore
it is said, "'That' comes from 'this,' and
'this' comes from 'that'"—which means
"that" and "this" give birth to one another.
Life arises from death and death from life.
What is inappropriate is seen by virtue of
what is appropriate. There is right because
of wrong, and wrong because of right.
Thus, the wise do not bother with these
distinctions but seek enlightenment from
heaven. So they see "this," but "this" is also
"that," and "that" is also "this." "That" has
elements of right and wrong, and "this" has
elements of right and wrong. Do they still
distinguish between "this" and "that," or
don't they? When there is no more separation between "this" and "that," it is called
the still-point of Tao. At the still-point in
the center of the circle, one can see the infinite in all things. Right is infinite; wrong
is also infinite. Therefore it is said, "Behold
the light beyond right and wrong."

To use one's fingers to demonstrate fingers not being fingers is not as good as using something else to demonstrate fingers not being fingers. Using horses to demonstrate horses not being horses is not as good as using something else to demonstrate horses not being horses. "Heaven and earth" are like a finger; "the ten thousand things" are like a horse.

What is acceptable is acceptable; what is not acceptable is not acceptable. A path is formed by walking on it. A thing has a name because of its being called something. Why is it like this? Because it is! Why is it not like that? Because it is not! Everything has its own nature and its own function. Nothing is without nature or function. Consider a small stalk or a great column, a leper or a beauty, things that are great or wicked, perverse, and strange. They are all one in Tao.

When there is separation, there is coming together. When there is coming together, there is dissolution. All things may become one, whatever their state of being. Only those who have transcended see this oneness, have no use for differences, and dwell in the constant. To be constant is to be useful. To be useful is to realize your true nature. Realization of your true nature is happiness. When you reach happiness, you are close to perfection. So you stop, yet do not know that you stop. This is Tao.

When you rack your brain trying to unify things without knowing that they are already one, it is called "three in the morning." What do I mean by "three in the morning"? A man who kept monkeys said to them, "You get three acorns in the morning and four in the evening." This made them all very angry. So he said, "How about four in the morning and three in the evening?"—and the monkeys were happy. The number of acorns was the same, but the different arrangement resulted in anger or pleasure. This is what I am talking about. Therefore, the wise harmonize right with wrong and rest in the balance of nature. This is called taking both sides at once.

以指喻指之非指不若以非指喻指之非指也
以馬喻馬之非馬不若以非馬喻馬之非馬也
天地一指也萬物一馬也可乎可不可乎不可
道行之而成
物謂之而然惡乎然然於然惡乎不然
不然於不然物固有所然物固有所可
無物不然無物不可故為是舉莛與楹
厲與西施恢恑憰怪道通為一
其分也成也其成也毀也凡物無成與毀復通為一
唯達者知通為一為是不用而寓諸庸
庸也者用也用也者通也通也者得也適得而幾矣因是已
已而不知其然謂之道勞神明為一而不知其同也謂之朝三
何謂朝三狙公賦芧曰朝三而暮四眾狙皆怒曰然則朝四而暮三
眾狙皆悅名實未虧而喜怒為用亦因是也是以聖人和之以是非
而休乎天鈞是之謂兩行

Among the ancients, knowledge was very deep. What is meant by deep? It reached back to the time when nothing existed. It was so deep, so complete, that nothing could be added to it. Then came people who distinguished between things but did not give them names. Later they labeled them but did not choose between right and wrong. When right and wrong appeared, Tao declined. With the fall of Tao, desire arose. Is there really rise and fall? When there is rise and fall, Chao Wen plays the lute. When there is no rise and fall, Chao Wen does not play the lute.

Chao Wen played the lute, Shia Kuang kept time with a baton, and Hui Tsu leaned on a stump and debated. Each of these three masters was nearly perfect in his own art. Their names will be remembered forevermore. Because they excelled, they were distinguished from others. Because they excelled, they wanted to enlighten others through their art. They tried to teach what could not be taught. This resulted in obscure discussions as to the nature of "hardness" and "whiteness." Their sons followed in their fathers' footsteps all their lives but accomplished nothing. However, if this can be called accomplishment, then even I have accomplished something. If this cannot be called accomplishment, then neither I nor others have accomplished anything. Therefore, the wise seek insight from chaos and doubt. Not making distinctions but dwelling on that which is unchanging is called clear vision.

古之人、其知有所至矣。惡乎至？有以為未始有物者、至矣、盡矣、不可以加矣。其次以為有物矣、而未始有封也。其次以為有封焉、而未始有是非也。是非之彰也、道之所以虧也。道之所以虧、愛之所以成。果且有成與虧乎哉？果且無成與虧乎哉？有成與虧、故昭氏之鼓琴也。無成與虧、故昭氏之不鼓琴也。昭文之鼓琴也、師曠之枝策也、惠子之據梧也、三子之知幾乎、皆其盛者也、故載之末年。唯其好之也、以異於彼、其好之也、欲以明之。彼非所明而明之、故以堅白之昧終。而其子又以文之綸終、終身無成。若是而可謂成乎、雖我無成、亦可謂成矣。若是而不可謂成乎、物與我無成也。是故滑疑之耀、聖人之所圖也。為是不用而寓諸庸、此之謂以明。

健

今日一別之於此之筆余為正顏字父与是石類字
類与石類相与石類刻与彼天以黑朱色色
諸當言之有收也在百年以石收や年
們年临夫来临石收也在百有有や年
有年临石天や石有青临夫来临石収
你宁有天矣空を石天之男収有百天や年
今我知之百語石矣空を百天や年
去男無之語乎天下莫大於秋语言真有語
直夫壽於孫子而彭租石天地変を臨小
空刀斯与我为一波と石一矣石为有言乎
波と語之一矣且石天言乎再言為二
二石一再三自此以徔巧樹石少石矣天凡乎
坡自无道万以玉於三宁沈自有道有乎
无道鳥母虽乎

Now I am going to tell you something. I don't know what heading it comes under, and whether or not it is relevant here, but it must be relevant at some point. It is not anything new, but I would like to say it.

There is a beginning. There is no beginning of that beginning. There is no beginning of that no beginning of beginning. There is something. There is nothing. There is something before the beginning of something and nothing, and something before that. Suddenly there is something and nothing. But between something and nothing, I still don't really know which is something and which is nothing. Now, I've just said something, but I don't really know whether I've said anything or not.

There is nothing in the world greater than the tip of a bird's feather, and Mount Tai is small. None have lived longer than a dead child, and old Peng Tsu died young. Heaven and earth grow together with me, and the ten thousand things and I are one. We are already one—what else is there to say? Yet I have just said that we are one, so my words exist also. The one and what I said about the one make two, and two and one make three. Thus it goes on and on. Even a skilled mathematician cannot reach the end, much less an ordinary person. If we proceed from nothing to something, we reach three. How much farther would it be going from something to something? Enough. Let us stop.

夫道未始有封、言未始有常、為是而有畛也。請言其畛。有左有右、有倫有義、有分有辯、有競有爭、此之謂八德。六合之外、聖人存而不論。六合之內、聖人論而不議。春秋經世先王之志、聖人議而不辯。故分也者、有不分也。辯也者、有不辯也。曰何也、聖人懷之、眾人辯之以相示也。故曰辯也者、有不見也。

At first Tao had no name. Words are not eternal. Because of words, there are distinctions. Let me describe these distinctions. There is left, and there is right; there is relationship, and there is duty; there is discernment, and there is discrimination; there is competition, and there is struggle. These are called the eight virtues.

Beyond the six realms of heaven, earth, and the four directions, the wise accept but do not discuss. Within the six realms, they discuss but do not pass judgment. In the Book of Spring and Autumn, the chronicle of the ancient kings, the wise pass judgment but do not question. When there is division, there is something which is not divided. When there is questioning, there is something beyond the question. Why is this? The wise keep their wisdom to themselves while ordinary people flaunt their knowledge in loud discussion. So I say, "Those who dispute do not see."

Great Tao is beyond description. Great argument uses no words. Great goodness is not kind. Great integrity is not incorruptible. Great courage is not aggressive. Tao that is manifest is not Tao. Words that argue miss the point. Perpetual kindness does not work. Obvious integrity is not believed. Aggressive courage will not win. These five are round and mellow, yet they may become square and inflexible.

Knowing enough to stop when one does not know is perfection.

Who can understand an argument that has no words and Tao that cannot be expressed? One who can understand this may be called the treasure house of heaven. Pour into it, and it will never be filled; pour out of it, and it will never be emptied. Yet no one knows why this is so. This is called the hidden light.

Long ago, Emperor Yao said to Shun, "I would like to attack the states of Tsung, Kuei, and Hsu Ao. This has been on my mind ever since I came to the throne. Why is this so?"

Shun said, "These three states eke out their existence in the weeds and bushes. Why bother? There was a time when ten suns rose all at once and the ten thousand things were illuminated. And yet how much greater is virtue than these suns!"

夫大道不称大辯不言大仁不仁大
廉不嗛大勇不忮道昭而不道
言辯而不及仁常而不成廉清而不信
勇忮而不成五者圓而幾向方矣
故知止其所不知至矣孰知不言之辯
不道之道若有能知此之謂天府
注焉而不滿酌焉而不竭而不知其所由來
此之謂葆光
故昔者堯問於舜曰我欲伐宗膾胥敖
南面而不釋然其故何也
舜曰夫三子者猶存乎蓬艾之間君不釋然何哉
昔年十日並出萬物皆照而况德之進乎日者乎

Yeh Chueh asked Wang I, "Do you know what is common to all things?"

"How should I know?" he replied.

"Do you know that you don't know?"

"How should I know?" he replied again.

"Then are all things not knowable?"

"How should I know? Still, let me put it this way: How do you know that what I say I know may not really be what I don't know? How do you know that what I say I don't know may not really be what I know? Now let me ask you something. If a person sleeps in a damp place, their back will ache and they will be half paralyzed. But does this happen to eels? If a person lives up in a tree, they will tremble with fright. But does this happen to monkeys? Of these three, who knows the right place to live? People eat flesh, deer eat grass, centipedes delight in worms, and owls and crows like mice. Of these four, which know what to eat? Monkeys mate with monkeys. Elk and deer run together, and eels play with fish.

"Mao Chiang and Li Chi were considered beautiful by people. But if fish saw them, they would dive to the bottom of the river. If birds saw them, they would fly off. If deer saw them, they would run away. Of these four, who recognizes real beauty?

"As I see it, the rules of goodness and wisdom and the paths of right and wrong are inextricably mingled and confused. How can I tell which is which?"

Yeh Chueh asked, "If you cannot distinguish between good and evil, then can the perfect person distinguish between them?"

Wang I replied, "Perfect people are spiritual. Though the great swamp burns, they will not feel the heat. Though the great rivers freeze, they will not feel the cold. Though thunderbolts split the mountains and gales shake the sea, they will have no fear. Such people can ride the clouds and mist, mount the sun and moon, and wander beyond the four seas. Life and death do not affect them. How much less will they be concerned with good and evil!"

Chu Chiao Tsu asked Chang Wu Tsu, "I have heard from Confucius that wise people are not troubled by worldly things. They do not look for gain or try to avoid loss; they seek nothing, and do not cling to Tao. Sometimes they say something without words, and sometimes their words say nothing. Thus they travel beyond the dusty world. Confucius thought these words to be mere fantasy. But I think this is the way of the unfathomable Tao. What do you think?"

Chang Wu Tsu replied, "These words would have confused even the Yellow Emperor,[7] so how could Confucius understand them? Moreover, you are too quick to draw conclusions. You see an egg, and immediately you listen for the crowing of a full-grown cock. You see a bow, and you look for a roast dove. Let me give you a rough explanation, but don't take this too literally. All right? How could anyone take his place beside the sun and moon, embrace the universe, be at one with all, refrain from interfering, and disregard the social order? Ordinary people labor and toil. The wise act without choosing. They experience ten thousand years as one age. To them the ten thousand things are what they are, yet they form a whole.

"How can I tell if love of life is not a delusion? How can I tell whether a person who fears death is not like a person who has left home and dreads returning? Lady Li was the daughter of a border guard of Ai. When the Duke of Chin first took her captive, she wept until her dress was soaked with tears. But once she was living in the Duke's palace, sharing his bed, and eating delicious food, she wondered why she had ever cried. How can I tell whether the dead are not amazed that they ever clung to life?

"Those who dream of a great feast may weep the next morning. Those who dream of weeping may enjoy the hunt the next day. While they dream, they do not know they are dreaming. They may even interpret their dreams while still dreaming. Only after they awake do they know it was a dream. By and by, there will be a great awakening; then we will know that this is all a great dream. All the while, the fools think they are awake, appearing to understand things, calling this one 'ruler' and that one 'herdsman.' How stupid! You and Confucius are both dreaming. When I say you are dreaming, I am dreaming too. These words may sound like double-talk. Yet after ten thousand generations, we will meet a great wise one who can explain all this. Or it may happen any time now."

予惡乎知說生之非惑邪予惡乎知惡死之非弱喪而不知歸者邪

麗之姬艾封人之子也晉國之始得之也涕泣沾襟

及其至於王所與王同筐床食芻豢而後悔其泣也

予惡乎知夫死者不悔其始之蘄生乎

夢飲酒者旦而哭泣夢哭泣者旦而田獵

方其夢也不知其夢也夢之中又占其夢焉覺而後知其夢也

且有大覺而後知此其大夢也

而愚者自以為覺竊竊然知之

君乎牧乎固哉丘也與女皆夢也

予謂女夢亦夢也

是其言也其名為弔詭

萬世之後而一遇大聖知其解者是旦暮遇之也

Suppose you and I argue. If you win and I lose, are you indeed right and I wrong? And if I win and you lose, am I right and you wrong? Are we both partly right and partly wrong? Are we both all right or both all wrong? If you and I cannot see the truth, other people will find it even harder.

Then whom shall I ask to be the judge? Shall I ask someone who agrees with you? If that one already agrees with you, how can that one be a fair judge? Shall I ask someone who agrees with me? If that one already agrees with me, how can that one be a fair judge? Shall I ask someone who agrees with both of us? If that one already agrees with both of us,

how can that one be a fair judge? Then if you and I and others cannot decide, shall we wait for still another? Waiting for changing opinions is like waiting for nothing. Seeing everything in relation to the heavenly cosmos and leaving the different viewpoints as they are, we may be able to live out our years.

What do I mean by seeing things in relation to the heavenly cosmos? Consider right and wrong, being and nonbeing. If right is indeed right, there need be no argument about how it is different from wrong. If being is really being, there need be no argument about how it is different from nonbeing. Forget time; forget distinction. Enjoy the infinite; rest in it.

既使我與若辯矣　若勝我　我不若勝　若果是也邪　我果非也邪　我勝若　若不吾勝　我果是也邪　而果非也邪　其或是也　其或非也邪　其俱是也　其俱非也邪　我與若不能相知也　則人固受其黮闇　吾誰使正之　使同乎若者正之　既與若同矣　惡能正之　使同乎我者正之　既同乎我矣　惡能正之　使異乎我與若者正之　既異乎我與若矣　惡能正之　使同乎我與若者正之　既同乎我與若矣　惡能正之　然則我與若與人俱不能相知也　而待彼也邪　化聲之相待　若其不相待　和之以天倪　因之以曼衍　所以窮年也　何謂和之以天倪　曰　是不是　然不然　是若果是也　則是之異乎不是也亦無辯　然若果然也　則然之異乎不然也亦無辯　忘年忘義　振於無竟　故寓諸無竟

許天賞

Shade said to Shadow, "A little while ago, you were moving; and now you are standing still. A little while ago, you were sitting down; and now you are getting up. Why all this indecision?"

Shadow replied, "Don't I have to depend on others to be what I am? Don't others also have to depend on something else to be what they are? My dependence is like that of the snake on his skin or of the cicada on his wings. How can I tell why I do this, or why I do that?"

Once upon a time, I, Chuang Tsu, dreamed I was a butterfly flying happily here and there, enjoying life without knowing who I was. Suddenly I woke up and I was indeed Chuang Tsu. Did Chuang Tsu dream he was a butterfly, or did the butterfly dream he was Chuang Tsu? There must be some distinction between Chuang Tsu and the butterfly. This is a case of transformation.

罔兩問景曰曩子行今子止曩子坐今子起何其无特操與景曰吾有待而然者邪吾所待又有待而然者邪吾待蛇蚹蜩翼邪惡識所以然惡識所以不然昔者莊周夢為胡蝶栩栩然胡蝶也自喻適志與不知周也俄然覺則蘧蘧然周也不知周之夢為胡蝶與胡蝶之夢為周與周與胡蝶則必有分矣此之謂物化

CHAPTER THREE

# THE SECRET OF GROWTH

吾生也有涯而知也无涯
以有涯随无涯殆已
已而为知者殆而已矣
为善无近名为恶无近刑
缘督以为经可以保身可以
可以养亲可以尽年
全生

Life has a limit, but knowledge is without limit.
For the limited to pursue the unlimited is futile.
To know this and still pursue knowledge is even more futile.
In doing good, avoid fame.
In doing evil, avoid punishment.

Thus, by pursuing the middle way, you may preserve your
body, fulfill your life, look after your parents, and live out
your years.

Prince Wen Hui's cook was carving up an ox. Every touch of his hand, every heave of his shoulder, every step of his foot, every thrust of his knee, with the slicing and parting of the flesh, and the zinging of the knife—all was in perfect rhythm, just like the Dance of the Mulberry Grove or a part in the Ching Shou symphony.

Prince Wen Hui remarked, "How wonderfully you have mastered your art."

The cook laid down his knife and said, "What your servant really cares for is Tao, which goes beyond mere art. When I first began to cut up oxen, I saw nothing but oxen. After three years of practicing, I no longer saw the ox as a whole. I now work with my spirit, not with my eyes. My senses stop functioning and my spirit takes over. I follow the natural grain, letting the knife find its way through the many hidden openings, taking advantage of what is there, never touching a ligament or tendon, much less a main joint.

"A good cook changes his knife once a year because he cuts, while a mediocre cook has to change his every month because he hacks. I've had this knife of mine for nineteen years and have cut up thousands of oxen with it, and yet the edge is as if it were fresh from the grindstone. There are spaces between the joints. The blade of the knife has no thickness. That which has no thickness has plenty of room to pass through these spaces. Therefore, after nineteen years, my blade is as sharp as ever. However, when I come to a difficulty, I size up the joint, look carefully, keep my eyes on what I am doing, and work slowly. Then with a very slight movement of the knife, I cut the whole ox wide open. It falls apart like a clod of earth crumbling to the ground. I stand there with the knife in my hand, looking about me with a feeling of accomplishment and delight. Then I wipe the knife clean and put it away."

"Well done!" said the Prince. "From the words of my cook, I have learned the secret of growth."

庖丁為文惠君解牛、手之所觸、肩之所倚、足之所履、膝之所踦、砉然嚮然、奏刀騞然、莫不中音。合於桑林之舞、乃中經首之會。

文惠君曰、譆、善哉、技蓋至此乎。

庖丁釋刀對曰、臣之所好者道也、進乎技矣。始臣之解牛之時、所見無非全牛者。三年之後、未嘗見全牛也。方今之時、臣以神遇而不以目視、官知止而神欲行。依乎天理、批大郤、導大窾、因其固然。技經肯綮之未嘗、而況大軱乎。良庖歲更刀、割也。族庖月更刀、折也。今臣之刀十九年矣、所解數千牛矣、而刀刃若新發於硎。彼節者有間、而刀刃者無厚。以無厚入有間、恢恢乎其於遊刃必有餘地矣。是以十九年而刀刃若新發於硎。雖然、每至於族、吾見其難為、怵然為戒、視為止、行為遲。動刀甚微、謋然已解、如土委地。提刀而立、為之四顧、為之躊躇滿志、善刀而藏之。

文惠君曰、善哉、吾聞庖丁之言、得養生焉。

公文軒見右師而驚曰是何人也惡乎介也天與其人與曰天也非人也天之生是使獨也人之貌有與也以是知其天也非人也澤雉十步一啄百步一飲不蘄畜乎樊中神雖王不善也

When Kung Wen Hsien saw the Commander of the Army, he was startled and exclaimed, "Who is this? Why does he have only one foot? Was it the work of heaven or of people?"

The Commander said, "It was the work of heaven, not people. Heaven made me one-footed. Heaven determines one's appearance; therefore I know it was heaven, not people. The pheasant in the marshes has to take ten steps in order to get one beakful of food, one hundred steps for one drink of water. Yet it doesn't want to be kept in a cage. Though it would be fed like a king, it would not be happy."

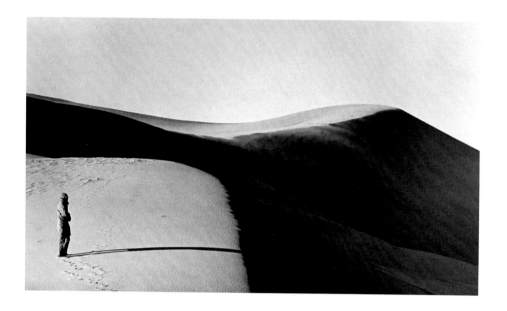

When Lao Tsu died, Chin Shih went to the funeral. He yelled three times and left.

A disciple said, "Were you not a friend of the Master?"

"Yes."

"Then is it proper to mourn him in this way?"

"Yes. When I first arrived, I thought his spirit was really there. Now I know it wasn't. When I went in to mourn, the old people were wailing as though they had lost their son. The young ones were crying as though they had lost their mother. Since they were all together, they talked and wept without any control. This is avoiding heaven, indulging in sentiment, ignoring what is natural. In the old days, it was called the crime of violating the law of nature.

"The Master came because it was time. He left because he followed the natural flow. Be content with the moment, and be willing to follow the flow; then there will be no room for grief or joy. In the old days this was called freedom from bondage. The wood is consumed but the fire burns on, and we do not know when it will come to an end."

芒種收秦生草之三□□雨出乃子日允夫子之女命日改
犹到不為若牛子不申日兆や要以面士人や哭乃みや
白云入帝中為有老女哭之為哭大世子
少年哭之為哭大世徃大斬以らこと心有不斬言而言以斬哭而哭矣
是賤遇天倍情忘此作学古今過之過天之刑
富夾夫女時や遇之夫子哭や
安時亦少以衰突余鈇みや
古寺沼号之帝之群龍
指寄稿於如女新
大侍やみもち尽々

人間世

CHAPTER FOUR

# HUMAN AFFAIRS

Yen Hui went to Confucius to say goodbye.

The Master asked, "Where are you going?"

"I am going to Wei."

"What are you going to do there?"

"I hear that the Prince of Wei is young and that he is arbitrary in his actions. He is not much concerned with his country and is not aware of his mistakes. He thinks nothing of people dying. The dead lie everywhere like thick grass in a swamp. The people have nowhere to turn. I've heard you, Master, say, 'Leave the country that is already well governed and go to a country that is in chaos.' At the door of a physician, there are many sick people. I would like to use your teaching to remedy the situation there."

Confucius said, "Ah! If you go there, you will only get into trouble. Tao must be pure. When something is added to it, there is confusion. When there is confusion, there is anxiety. With anxiety, there is no hope. The wise ones of old realized Tao in themselves before they offered it to others. If you are not certain that you have it in yourself, how can you change a tyrant's action?

"Besides, do you know how virtue degenerates and how learning arises? Virtue is consumed by fame. Learning is born of contention. Fame causes people to fight with one another. Learning is the weapon for the struggle. Both can be evil instruments. They are not the means to perfection. Though you are highly virtuous and trustworthy, if you do not understand the people's spirits, and though you are famous and do not compete, if you do not understand the people's minds, but instead go to a tyrant and lecture him on goodness, ethical behavior, measures, and standards, you are just using the failings of others to demonstrate your own superiority. This is deliberately hurting other people. One who hurts others will in turn be hurt. You will probably end up in trouble."

顏回見仲尼請行曰奚之曰將之衛曰奚為焉曰回聞衛君其年壯其行獨輕用其國而不見其過輕用民死死者以國量乎澤若蕉民其無如矣回嘗聞之夫子曰治國去之亂國就之醫門多疾願以所聞思其則庶幾其國有瘳乎仲尼曰譆若殆往而刑耳夫道不欲雜雜則多多則擾擾則憂憂而不救古之至人先存諸己而後存諸人所存於己者未定何暇至於暴人之所行且若亦知夫德之所蕩而知之所為出乎哉德蕩乎名知出乎爭名也者相軋也知也者爭之器也二者凶器非所以盡行也且德厚信矼未達人氣名聞不爭未達人心而強以仁義繩墨之言術暴人之前者是以人惡有其美也命之曰菑人菑人者人必反菑之若殆為人菑夫

"If indeed the Prince likes good people and hates bad people, why would you try to change him? If he does not, you would be better off saying nothing; for if you do speak, the Prince will expose your weak points and win the argument. You will look confused and ashamed; you will find one excuse after another and you will seem to yield. Your mind will be molded to his way of thinking. This is putting out fire with fire, adding water to a flood; it is called adding to the excess. If you start by giving in, there will be no end to your concessions. And if you speak out strongly against him, he will not listen to you and will undoubtedly put you to death.

"In ancient times, Chieh killed Kuan Lung Pang and Chou killed Prince Pi Kan. These two victims were virtuous men who tried hard to comfort and aid the common people. In this way they offended their superiors. Their rulers had them put to death because of their goodness. This was the result of seeking fame for their virtue. Many years ago, Yao attacked the states of Tsung Chi and Hsu Ao; Yu attacked Yuo Hu. These nations were laid into waste and destroyed, their rulers killed. For all of them were constantly at war in an effort to win more. They were all seekers of fame and wealth. Have you never heard of them? Even the wise ones cannot deal with fame and wealth. So how can you? However, you must have something else in mind. Come tell me what it is."

是苗而悦賢而惡不肖思用而求有以盡其藏也无諱其愧將乘人而鬪其捷
而自獲榮乎而色情乎乙哮將拮已心且用已巧以攻之水微火
沈拔水名乞曰巫厥多順乎夫宗若弱以不信貞言心孰猶孤其人已戌
目著氏築殺闡龍逢紂殺王子比干是岂修夫身以不德附人之戌
以下端夫夫也故夫君因乎修以損之言岂苦知夫苦以慕技胄放
患乃有危圍國虚廉身而創載其用兵以曰矣寅無己是岂岂求名乎苦
而猶乃周之事名岂在聖人之所不能那也而況若耳衡乎苦岂有以
寄以浩邦未

Yen Hui said, "If I am detached and self-assured, persevering and of one mind, won't that work?"

"What! How can that work? You may put on a brave show, but your uncertainty will appear on your face as it would with anyone else. This prince takes pleasure in exploiting the feelings of others. He cannot even practice the ordinary virtues. How do you expect him to appreciate the higher virtues? He will be obstinate and unbending. Outwardly he may agree, but there will be no inward change of heart. How can you succeed in that way?"

"Well then, I will be inwardly firm and outwardly compliant. I will arm myself with examples from antiquity. Being inwardly firm, I will be a follower of heaven. Being a follower of heaven, I know that the Prince and I are both sons of heaven. So, why should I mind whether or not people approve of my words? People call this being childlike. This is what I call being a follower of heaven.

"By being outwardly compliant, I am a follower of men. Lifting the tablet, kneeling, bending, and bowing—this is how a minister behaves. All people do this. Why shouldn't I? Do as others do, and there is no trouble! This is what I call being a follower of others.

"By observing the customs, I will be following ancient tradition. Though my words may be chiding and critical, they will not be my own words but the words of the sages. So I need not be afraid of speaking out. This is what I mean by following tradition. Will that work?"

Confucius said, "How could that work? You have too many plans. They are fine but not appropriate. These preconceived ideas probably won't get you into trouble, but that is as far as they go. How can you possibly influence him? You are still too rigid in your thinking."

顔曰端而虚勉而一則可乎曰惡惡可夫以陽而充孔揚
采色不定常人之所不違因案人之所感以求容與其心名之曰
日漸之德不成而況大德乎將執而不化外合而内不訾其庸詎可乎
然則我内直而外曲成而上比内直者與天為徒
與天為徒者知天子之與己皆天之所子
而獨以己言蘄乎而人善之蘄乎而人不善之邪
若然者人謂之童子是之謂與天為徒
外曲者與人之為徒也擎跪曲拳
人臣之禮也人皆為之吾敢不為邪
為人之所為者人亦無疵焉是之謂與人為徒
成而上比者與古為徒其言雖教讁之實也
古之有也非吾有也若然者雖直而不病
是之謂與古為徒若是則可乎
仲尼曰惡惡可大多政法而不諜
雖固亦無罪雖然止是耳矣夫胡可以及化
猶師心者也

Yen Hui said, "That is all I can think of. May I ask what to do?"

Confucius said, "You must fast. I'll tell you why. Is it easy to work from preconceived ideas? Heaven frowns on those who think it is easy."

Yen Hui said, "My family is poor. I have neither drunk wine nor eaten meat for many months. Can this be considered fasting?"

Confucius replied, "That is the fasting one does for sacrificial ceremonies, not the fasting of the mind."

Yen Hui said, "May I ask what is fasting of the mind?"

Confucius said, "Your will must be one. Do not listen with your ears but with your mind. Do not listen with your mind but with your vital energy. Ears can only hear, mind can only think, but vital energy is empty, receptive to all things. Tao abides in emptiness. Emptiness is the fasting of mind."

Yen Hui said, "Before I heard all this, I was certain that I was Hui. Now that I've heard it, I am no longer Hui. Can this be called emptiness?"

Confucius said, "That is it. Let me explain. You can enter this man's service, but do not thrust yourself forward. If he listens, then speak. If not, be silent. Leave no opening, and you will not be harmed. Be always at one and accept whatever happens. Then you are close to success. If you do not move, then it is easy to remain unnoticed. But it is hard to walk without touching the ground. It is easy to be a hypocrite in your dealings with people. It is hard to be a hypocrite in your dealings with heaven.

"You understand how to fly using wings, but you have not yet seen how to fly without them. You understand how to act from knowledge, but you have not yet seen how to act from not-knowing. Look at empty space. It is in emptiness that light is born. There is happiness in stillness. Lack of stillness is called sitting while wandering. If you are open to everything you see and hear, and allow this to act through you, even gods and spirits will come to you, not to speak of people. This is the transformation of the ten thousand things, the secret of the wise kings Yu and Shun, the constant practice of Fu Hsi and Chi Chu. It is even more useful for ordinary people."

顏回曰吾無以進矣敢問其方仲尼曰齋吾將語若有而為之其易邪易之者皞天不宜顏回曰回之家貧唯不飲酒不茹葷者數月矣如此則可以為齋乎曰是祭祀之齋非心齋也回曰敢問心齋仲尼曰若一志無聽之以耳而聽之以心無聽之以心而聽之以氣聽止於耳心止於符氣也者虛而待物者也唯道集虛虛者心齋也顏回曰回之未始得使實自回也得使之也未始有回也可謂虛乎夫子曰盡矣吾語若若能入遊其樊而無感其名入則鳴不入則止無門無毒一宅而寓於不得已則幾矣絕迹易無行地難為人使易以偽為天使難以偽聞以有翼飛者矣未聞以無翼飛者也聞以有知知者矣未聞以無知知者也瞻彼闋者虛室生白吉祥止止夫且不止是之謂坐馳夫徇耳目內通而外於心知鬼神將來舍而況人乎是萬物之化也禹舜之所紐也伏戲几蘧之所行終而況散焉者乎

Tsu Kao, the Duke of She, was being sent to the state of Chi on a mission, and went first to consult Confucius, saying, "The King is dispatching me on a very important mission. Chi will probably treat me with great respect but will be slow to start our discussions. Even an ordinary person is not easily hurried, much less a feudal lord. I am very worried. You always said to me, 'In all matters, great or small, few will succeed without following Tao.' If this mission is not successful, I shall be criticized. If it is successful, I will be troubled by confusion and anxiety. Only a wise person is not concerned with results—and is therefore unaffected by the outcome. I eat simple, unspiced food, so I never need cooling drinks. I received these orders one morning, and by the evening I was drinking vast quantities of water. Am I not feverish? I have not yet seen the actual situation and already I am troubled by anxiety and confusion. If I do not succeed, I am bound to be criticized. I am in a double bind. This is beyond my capacity as a minister. Will you tell me what to do?"

葉子高好龍於牖雕以寫龍鑿以寫龍屋室雕文以寫龍於是天龍聞而下之窺頭於牖施尾於堂葉公見之棄而還走失其魂魄五色無主是葉公非好龍也好夫似龍而非龍者也今臣聞君好士故不遠千里之外以見君七日而君不禮君非好士也好夫似士而非士者也

Confucius replied, "In the affairs of the world, two universal principles may be observed: one is the natural order and the other is duty. It is natural for a son to love his parents; this cannot be erased from his heart. It is duty for one to serve one's sovereign; everywhere one goes there will be a sovereign. Within heaven and earth, there is no escape. That is why they are called universal principles. Therefore, to honor one's parents, wherever one may be, is the fullness of devotion. To serve one's sovereign willingly, whatever happens, is the perfect loyalty. To serve one's own mind, unmoved by sadness or joy, accepting whatever happens, is the true virtue. Being a son or a subject, there is always something unavoidable that one has to do. Do what has to be done and give no thought to yourself; then you will not have time to think about loving life and hating death. Continue in this way and all will go well.

"Let me tell you something else I have heard. If states have close ties, their mutual trust is demonstrated by deeds. If they are far apart, their good faith has to be renewed with words in the form of messages. But carrying messages of delight or anger between two parties is the most difficult thing in the world. When they are both pleased, there is bound to be exaggeration of flattery; when they are both angry, there is bound to be exaggeration of criticism. Exaggeration leads away from truth. Without truth, there will be no trust. When there is no trust, the messengers will be in danger. Therefore, it is said, 'Speak the truth and do not exaggerate; then you will not be harmed.'

仲尼曰天下有大戒二其一命也其一義也子之愛親命也
不可解於心臣之事君義也無適而非君也無所逃於天地之間
是之謂大戒是以夫事其親者不擇地而安之孝之至也
夫事其君者不擇事而安之忠之盛也自事其心者
哀樂不易施乎前知其不可奈何而安之若命德之至也
為人臣子者固有所不得已行事之情而忘其身
何暇至於悅生而惡死夫子其行可矣
丘請復以所聞凡交近則必相靡以信遠則必忠之以言
言必或傳之夫傳兩喜兩怒之言天下之難者也
夫兩喜必多溢美之言
兩怒必多溢惡之言凡溢之類妄
妄則其信之也莫莫則傳言者殃
故法言曰傳其常情無傳其溢言則幾乎全

且以巧鬪力者將才陽常多陰少以九飲沈比將宰常宰乱大至剛多柔少凡已志者
扎虫涂常宰宰鄙头作也将其实志忌以色
風波や行衣实变心風波鳥以幼実变忌以色
故忽没無由巧言倜辭獸然不撣音氣息兼此
於是尽心腐刺杖大己則必有不前忘之而不知去然也
苟而石知去矣熟知去欢也
過度二宴や當令功弦了善關在久
悉同公居好ののて塙ても
正未乘凿游心论仁り心言り申
此其難4
玉矣何作石拔や其岩子没一即

"Moreover, when wrestlers pit their strength against each other, they begin in a lighthearted, open frame of mind but they usually end up looking angry. At the height of the contest, many crafty tricks are played. When people drink during ceremonies, they start off in an orderly manner and usually finish in disarray. At the height of the party, fun becomes chaos. So it is with all things. They begin in good faith and end up in meanness. What was simple in the beginning becomes grotesque in the end. Words are like the wind and the waves; action involves the risk of gain or loss. The wind and the waves are easily set in motion; risk can easily turn into real danger. Hence, anger comes from nothing more than clever words and half truths. When animals face death, they do not care what noises they make. They growl fiercely and snarl, and then they attack. In the same way, if a person is pushed too far, that person turns and strikes without knowing why. If one does not know why, who knows where it will lead? Therefore, it is said, 'Neither deviate from your instructions, nor hurry to finish.' Do not force things. It is dangerous to deviate from instructions or push for completion. It takes a long time to do

a thing properly. Once you do something wrong, it may be too late to change it. Can you afford to be careless?

"So then, flow with whatever may happen and let your mind be free; stay centered by accepting whatever you are doing. This is the ultimate. How else can you carry out your task? It is best to leave everything to work naturally, though this is not easy."

Yen Ho was about to become tutor of the Crown Prince, the son of Duke Ling of the state of Wei. He went to consult Chu Po Yu, saying, "Here is someone who is naturally violent. If I let him remain undisciplined, the state will be in danger. If I try to correct him, I shall endanger myself. He knows enough to see the faults of others, but not to see his own. Under these circumstances, what shall I do?"

Chu Po Yu replied, "That is a good question! Be on guard, be careful, and be sure that you yourself are acting appropriately. Appear to be flexible but maintain harmony within. However, there is danger in doing these two things. While being flexible, sure to remain centered. While maintaining harmony within, do not display it openly. If you are too flexible and lose your center, then you will be overcome and destroyed, and you will collapse. If you try to demonstrate your composure, you will be criticized and slandered, called a devil. If he wants to be a child, be a child with him. If he wants to act strangely, act strangely with him. If he wants to be reckless, be reckless with him. Then you can reach him and bring him back to his senses.

"Do you know the story of the praying mantis? It raised its arm to stop an approaching carriage unaware that this was beyond its power. Such was its high opinion of itself. Watch out and be careful. If you offend the Prince by showing off your own talents, you court disaster.

"Do you know how tiger trainers work? They do not risk feeding the tigers live animals for fear of arousing their ferocity as they kill. They do not risk feeding them whole animals for fear of arousing their anger as they tear them apart. They know when the tigers are hungry and when they are full; thereby the trainers are in touch with their fierce nature. Tigers are a different species from humans, yet by observing their ways, one can train them to be gentle. Tigers will kill only when aroused.

"A person with a passion for horses catches the manure in a basket and the piss in a jar. If a mosquito or a fly lands on the horse and one brushes it off too abruptly, then the horse will break its bit, hurt that person's head, and crack their ribs. Such a person has good intentions, but overdoes it. Can you afford to be careless?"

汝ニ知ル夫蟷螂や恐ス背ニ当ヲ車軸ヲ知ス勝任や目ヲ天才ニ夫ヲや
戒ニ慎ニ慎代ニ未セ心死ニ化二ル年
比ニ知ス夫ニ宇実ヲナス助ニ生物ヲテ子殺ニニ恐やニ敢ニ全世ニ
子女冲ニニ恐や時ヲ飢餓ヲテ恐心侯ニ思人黒数ニ懼ニテ己ヲ噴や
比天殺ヲ返ヤ
夫学馬ニ隹臥隔適有罹ニ童僕緣ニ将ニ時ニ肚衝明首石囲
意有ヤ己ニ宇宙有ルコア不慎和

Shih the carpenter was on his way to the state of Chi. When he got to Chu Yuan, he saw an oak tree by the village shrine. The tree was large enough to shade several thousand oxen and was a hundred spans around. It towered above the hilltops with its lowest branches eighty feet from the ground. More than ten of its branches were big enough to be made into boats. There were crowds of people as in a marketplace. The master carpenter did not even turn his head but walked on without stopping.

His apprentice took a long look, then ran after Shih the carpenter and said, "Since I took up my ax and followed you, master, I have never seen timber as beautiful as this. But you do not even bother to look at it, and walk on without stopping. Why is this?"

Shih the carpenter replied, "Stop! Say no more! That tree is useless. A boat made from it would sink, a coffin would soon rot, a tool would split, a door would ooze sap, and a beam would have termites. It is worthless timber and is of no use. That is why it has reached such a ripe old age."

匠石之齊至於曲轅
見櫟社樹其大蔽數千牛
絜之百圍其高臨山十仞而後有枝
其可以為舟者旁十數觀者如市
匠伯不顧遂行不輟弟子厭觀之走及匠石曰
自吾執斧斤以隨夫子未嘗見材如此其美也
先生不肯視行不輟何邪
曰已矣勿言之矣散木也以為舟則沈
以為棺槨則速腐以為門戶則液樠
以為柱則蠹是不材之木也
無所可用故能若是之壽

After Shih the carpenter had returned home, the sacred oak appeared to him in a dream, saying, "What are you comparing me with? Are you comparing me with useful trees? There are cherry, apple, pear, orange, citron, pomelo, and other fruit trees. As soon as the fruit is ripe, the trees are stripped and abused. Their large branches are split, and the smaller ones torn off. Their life is bitter because of their usefulness. That is why they do not live out their natural lives but are cut off in their prime. They attract the attentions of the common world. This is so for all things. As for me, I have been trying for a long time to be useless. I was almost destroyed several times. Finally I am useless, and this is very useful to me. If I had been useful, could I have ever grown so large?

"Besides, you and I are both things. How can one thing judge another thing? What does a dying and worthless man like you know about a worthless tree?"

Shih the carpenter awoke and tried to understand his dream.

His apprentice said, "If it had so great a desire to be useless, why does it serve as a shrine?"

Shih the carpenter said, "Hush! Stop talking! It is just pretending to be one so that it will not be hurt by those who do not know it is useless. If it had not become a sacred tree, it would probably have been cut down. It protects itself in a different way from ordinary things. We will miss the point if we judge it in the ordinary way."

匠石歸櫟社見夢曰
女將惡乎比予哉若將比予於文木邪
夫柤梨橘柚果蓏之屬實熟則剝
剝則辱大枝折小枝泄
此以其能苦其生者也
故不終其天年而中道夭
自掊擊於世俗者也物莫不若是
且予求无所可用久矣幾死乃今得之為予大用
使予也而有用且得有此大也邪
且也若與予也皆物也奈何哉其相物也
而幾死之散人又惡知散木
匠石覺而診其夢弟子曰趣取无用則為社何邪
曰密若無言彼亦直寄焉以為不知己者詬厲也
不為社者且幾有翦乎
且也彼其所保與眾異而以義譽之不亦遠乎

Nan Po Tsu Chi was wandering in the Shang Hills when he caught sight of a huge, extraordinary tree. A thousand four-horse chariots could have rested in its shade. Tsu Chi said, "What kind of tree is this? It must be very special wood." He looked up and saw that the smaller branches were gnarled and twisted, and could not be used for beams or rafters. He looked down and saw that the great trunk was curved and knotted, and could not be used for coffins. When he tasted a leaf, it burned his mouth; when he sniffed it, he became intoxicated and for three days acted as if he were drunk. Tsu Chi said, "Indeed, this tree is good for nothing. No wonder it grew so big. That is how it is! Holy men treasure this worthlessness."

Ching Shih in the province of Sung is a good place for growing catalpa, cypress, and mulberry trees. Those trees that attain the girth of a span or more are cut down to make monkey perches. Those of three or four spans are cut down to make beams for tall, elegant houses. Those of seven or eight spans are cut down to make side boards for the coffins of aristocratic and rich merchant families. So, these trees never achieve their full stature but fall in their prime under the blows of the ax. Such are the hazards of being useful.

In the same way, oxen with white foreheads, pigs with turned-up snouts, and people with piles may not be sacrificed to the River God.[8] Some believe these creatures bring bad luck. Holy ones, however, believe they are very fortunate.

南伯子綦游乎商之丘，見大木焉有異，結駟千乘，隱將芘其所藾。子綦曰：此何木也哉？此必有異材夫！仰而視其細枝，則拳曲而不可以為棟梁；俯而視其大根，則軸解而不可以為棺槨；咶其葉，則口爛而為傷；嗅之，則使人狂酲，三日而不已。子綦曰：此果不材之木也，以至於此其大也。嗟乎神人，以此不材。宋有荊氏者，宜楸柏桑。其拱把而上者，求狙猴之杙者斬之；三圍四圍，求高名之麗者斬之；七圍八圍，貴人富商之家求樿傍者斬之。故未終其天年，而中道之夭於斧斤，此材之患也。故解之以牛之白顙者，與豚之亢鼻者，與人有痔病者，不可以適河。此皆巫祝以知之矣，所以為不祥也，此乃神人之所以為大祥也。

支離疏者頤隱於臍肩高於頂會撮指天五管在上兩髀為脅
挫鍼治繲足以餬口鼓筴播精足以食十人上徵武士
則支離攘臂而遊於其間上有大役
則支離以有常疾不受功
上與病者粟則受三鐘與十束薪
夫支離其形者猶足以養其身
終其天年
又況支離其德者乎

There was once a hunchback called Shu. His chin rested on his navel, his shoulders rose up over his head, and his neck bone pointed to the sky. His five vital organs were upside down, and his hips were level with his ribs. By sewing and taking in laundry, he made enough to feed himself. By winnowing and sifting grain, he earned enough to support ten people. When the authorities were raising an army, he came and went without having to hide. When a big public project was planned, he was assigned no work because he was a chronic invalid. When the government was giving free grain to the sick, he received three measures and ten bundles of firewood. If those whose bodies are strange can take care of themselves and live to the end of their natural lives, how much easier it is for a person with strange behavior.

孔子適楚楚狂接輿遊其門曰鳳兮鳳兮
何如德之衰也來世不可待往世不可追也
天下有道聖人成焉天下無道聖人生焉
方今之時僅免刑焉福輕乎羽莫之知載
禍重乎地莫之知避已乎已乎臨人以德
殆乎殆乎畫地而趨迷陽迷陽
无傷吾行吾行卻曲无傷吾足
山木自寇也膏火自煎也
桂可食故伐之漆可用故割之
人皆知有用之用而莫知无用之用也

When Confucius was in the state of Chu, the madman of Chu, Chieh Yu, stood at his gate and cried, "O phoenix, O phoenix, how virtue has declined! One cannot wait for the future. One cannot chase after the past. When Tao is in the world, the wise person achieves perfection; when Tao is absent, the wise merely bide their time. In times like these, the best you can do is to stay out of trouble. Happiness is as light as a feather, but nobody knows how to bear it. Calamity is as heavy as the earth, but nobody knows how to avoid it.

"Enough! Enough of this confronting people with virtue! Beware! Beware of trudging down this marked path. Oh, thorns, thorns! You do not block my way. My path twists around you. You do not hurt my feet.

"The mountain trees ask to be chopped down. Fat added to the fire consumes itself. The cinnamon tree is edible, so it is cut down. The lacquer tree is useful, so it is slashed. Everyone knows the usefulness of the useful, but no one knows the usefulness of the useless."

CHAPTER FIVE

# SIGNS OF FULL VIRTUE

In the state of Lu, there was a man named Wang Tai who had but one foot. He had as many followers as Confucius. Chang Chi asked Confucius, "This Wang Tai is a cripple, yet he has as many followers in the state of Lu as you do. When he stands up, he does not teach. When he sits down, he utters no word. People go to him empty, and come back full. Is there such a thing as teaching without words? Can the mind be perfect while the body is deformed? What kind of man is he?"

Confucius said, "This man is wise. It is just that I have been a little slow in going to see him. I myself am going to make him my teacher. Why shouldn't all of you who are my disciples do the same? I shall bring the whole world, not just the state of Lu, to sit at his feet."

Chang Chi said, "He is a cripple, yet he can be your teacher. He must be quite an extraordinary man. What is unique about the way he uses his mind?"

Confucius said, "Death and life are important, yet they do not affect him. Heaven and earth may collapse, yet he remains unmoved. He perceives the true reality and is not affected by external appearances. He lets things change naturally, and so he holds fast to the roots."

Chang Chi said, "What do you mean?"

Confucius said, "If we observe things from the point of view of their differences, liver and gall are as unlike one another as the state of Chu in the west and the state of Yueh in the east. If we see that which is the same in all things, then the ten thousand things are one. He who sees things in this light is not distracted by what reaches him through his ears and his eyes but lets his mind follow the natural harmony. He sees all things as one and is not troubled by loss. To him, the loss of his foot is just like throwing away so much dirt."

常季自得る之心実知今志心以志心以志心以去真心
物なる其那之郡仲也きり人莫隨打流水
而隨打止水唯此獨己留心學命於坤
以於柏獨や在冬夏青青學命於天
唯聖獨や止幸神止去以也眾生
夫得將之微羅之家肩七人旅の手九章
將我私る所自安女宗施君牛
雲流雪天地充乃動有寓之骸
家子月一私之所を心声喜死を卑
徒見揮日宗登修人身層巢や
徒且何旨以知る了す

Chang Chi said, "He is for himself. He uses his knowledge to perfect his mind and he uses his mind to attain the universal mind. Why do people turn to him in such numbers?"

Confucius said, "People cannot see their reflection in running water but only in still water. Only that which is still in itself can still the seekers of stillness. Of those things that receive life from the earth, the pine and cypress trees alone stand out. They remain green summer and winter long. Of those that receive life from heaven, the wise King Shun alone was upright. Being fortunate, he was able to order his own life and thus order the lives of others. Holding fast to one's own roots is the foundation of courage. A single brave soldier may overcome nine armies. If he can do this simply because he wants recognition, how much more can be done by one who rules heaven and earth, who embraces the ten thousand things, who dwells only for a time in the body, whose ears and eyes are just for forming images, who unifies all knowledge and never experiences death? He will soon, at a time of his own choosing, leave the dusty world and rise to another level. The world will naturally follow him. Why should he be concerned with the affairs of the world?"

Shen Tu Chia had had his foot cut off as punishment. He and Tsu Chan, the Prime Minister of the state of Cheng, were students of Po Hun Wu Jen.

Tsu Chan said to Shen Tu Chia, "If I leave first, you will stay behind. If you leave first, I will stay behind."

The next day they were once more sitting together in the hall on the same mat. Tsu Chan said to Shen Tu Chia, "If I leave first, you will stay behind. If you leave first, I will stay behind. Now that I am about to leave, will you stay behind or not? I might add that when you see me, you do not even move out of the way. Perhaps you think that you are the equal of a Prime Minister?"

Shen Tu Chia said, "In our master's house is there such a thing as a Prime Minister? Perhaps you are proud of being a Prime Minister and being above everybody. I have heard that if a mirror is bright, dust and dirt will not settle on it. If they do, then it is not really bright. If one remains with a wise person for a long time, one will be without faults. Now, you are seeking great things from our master, yet you still talk like this. Is this proper?"

申徒嘉，兀者也，而與鄭子產同師於伯昏無人。子產謂申徒嘉曰：「我先出則子止，子先出則我止。」其明日，又與合堂同席而坐。子產謂申徒嘉曰：「我先出則子止，子先出則我止。今我將出，子可以止乎？其未邪？且子見執政而不違，子齊執政乎？」申徒嘉曰：「先生之門，固有執政焉如此哉？子而說子之執政而後人者也？聞之曰：鑑明則塵垢不止，止則不明也。久與賢人處則無過。今子之所取大者，先生也，而猶出言若是，不亦過乎！」

Tsu Chan said, "Take a look at yourself! You still think that you can be as good as Yao. Examine your virtues. Perhaps you will have cause to reflect."

Shen Tu Chia said, "Those who justify their faults to avoid punishment are many, and those who do not justify their faults and refuse to be spared are few. But only the virtuous person can resign themself to the inevitable and accept it as fate. Those who wander in front of archer Yi's target will be hit. If they do not get hit, it is fate. Many people who have both feet laugh at me for having only one. I used to explode with anger. Since I came to study with the Master, I have changed completely. Perhaps he has washed me clean with his goodness. I have been with the Master for nineteen years, and I have never been aware of having only one foot. Now, you and I are supposed to be concerned with our inner selves and yet you pay attention to my external body. Is this proper?"

Tsu Chan was disconcerted, his expression changed, and he asked Shen Tu Chia to say no more.

子產曰子哉曰得其所哉故君子可欺以其方
故信嘉曰自始舍之圉圉焉少則洋洋焉攸
然而逝予既烹而食之若得命哉予遊於之釜中
故君子也予既而食反命焉令校人畜之事乃還
校人烹之反命曰始舍之圉圉焉少則洋洋焉
昔者有饋生魚於鄭子產子產使校人畜之
子產誠然洛焉而既日子之言乃孫

魯有兀者叔山无趾踵見仲尼仲尼曰子不謹前既犯患若是矣雖今來何及矣无趾曰吾唯不知務而輕用吾身吾是以亡足今吾來也猶有尊足者存吾是以務全之也夫天无不覆地无不載吾以夫子為天地安知夫子之猶若是也孔子曰丘則陋矣夫子胡不入乎請講以所聞无趾出孔子曰弟子勉之夫无趾兀者也猶務學以復補前行之惡而況全德之人乎无趾語老聃曰孔丘之於至人其未邪彼何賓賓以學子為彼且蘄以諔詭幻怪之名聞不知至人之以是為己桎梏邪老聃曰胡不直使彼以死生為一條以可不可為一貫者解其桎梏其可乎无趾曰天刑之安可解

There was a cripple in Lu named Shu Shan No-toes. He came walking on his heels to see Confucius. Confucius said, "You did not take care. You committed a crime and brought this trouble upon yourself. What is the use of coming to me now?"

No-toes said, "I didn't know how to behave properly, and took my body lightly, so I lost my toes. I have come here with something more precious than toes, and it is this which I seek to preserve. There is nothing that heaven does not cover. There is nothing that earth does not sustain. I thought that you, Master, were like heaven and earth. How was I to know that you would receive me this way?"

Confucius said, "It was stupid of me. Why don't you come in! Let us talk."

But No-toes walked out.

Confucius said, "This is a good lesson, disciples! A toeless cripple is still willing to atone for his past misdeeds. How much more can be done by those who haven't had such bad luck?"

No-toes went to see Lao Tsu and said, "Is Confucius not yet a perfect man? Why does he keep imitating you? He is trying to gain a reputation by pretending to know strange and extraordinary things. He does not know that real wise ones look upon these as cuffs and fetters."

Lao Tsu said, "Why don't you simply make him see that life and death are one thread, the same line viewed from different sides—and thus free him from his cuffs and fetters? Is that possible?"

No-toes said, "If heaven wants to punish him, who can free him?"

Duke Ai of Lu asked Confucius, "In Wei, there was an ugly man by the name of Ai Tai To. Yet the men around him thought so much of him, they could never leave him. When young ladies saw him, they told their parents that they would rather be his concubines than other men's wives. There were ten or more such cases. He never tried to lead others but always went along with people. He was never in the position of a ruler who could protect people's lives. He was not a wealthy man who could fill people's bellies. Moreover, he was hideous enough to scare everything under heaven. He agreed with people but never persuaded them. He knew only what happened in the place where he lived. Yet both men and women sought his company. There must have been something extraordinary about him, I thought. So I summoned him for an interview, and indeed he was frighteningly ugly. Yet within the first month that he was with me, I began to see that there was something in that man, and within a year I completely trusted him. As my state needed a Prime Minister, I offered him the position. He was reluctant to give a reply, and was evasive as though he wanted to refuse. That made me feel ashamed, and finally I handed over the government to him. Soon after that, he went away and left me.

I was so sad, it was as if I were in mourning. I no longer had anyone with whom I could share the joy of my state. What kind of man was that?"

Confucius said, "Once when I was on a mission to the state of Chu, I saw some little pigs suckling their dead mother. After a while, they suddenly looked at her. Then they all ran away and left her because she did not look back at them. She was no longer like themselves. What they loved in their mother was not her body but that which made her body alive. When a man is killed in battle and is buried, he has no use for medals. When a man has no feet, he does not care about shoes. Both men have lost something essential. The King's concubines do not trim their nails or pierce their ears. When a man is newly married, he stays away from his official duties and is not sent on missions. Such is the importance of keeping the body whole. How much more important to preserve virtue. Now, Ai Tai To said nothing and was trusted. He achieved nothing and was loved. So someone offered him the government, and was only afraid that he would refuse. He must have achieved full harmony without any outward manifestation of virtue."

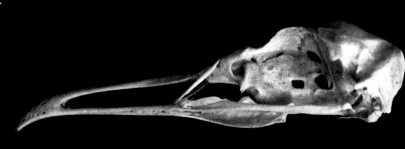

Duke Ai asked, "What do you mean by achieving full harmony?"

Confucius said, "Life and death, profit and loss, failure and success, poverty and wealth, value and worthlessness, praise and blame, hunger and thirst, cold and heat—these are natural changes in the order of things. They alternate with each other like day and night. No one knows where one ends and the other begins. Therefore, they should not disturb our peace or enter into our souls. Live so that you are at ease, in harmony with the world, and full of joy. Day and night, share the springtime with all things, thus creating the seasons in your own heart. This is called achieving full harmony."

"And what is this lack of outward manifestation of virtue?"

Confucius said, "Balance is the perfect state of still water. Let that be our model. It remains quiet within and is not disturbed on the surface. Virtue is the attainment of perfect harmony. Because virtue has no outward form, nothing can escape from it."

Later, Duke Ai told this to Ming Tsu, saying, "When I first faced south and took the reins of government, guiding the people and caring for their lives, I thought that I was doing my utmost as a ruler. Now that I have heard the words of a perfect man, I am afraid that there is no substance to what I am doing. I have foolishly squandered my energy and am ruining my country. Confucius and I are no longer related as subject and ruler but as spiritual companions."

Clubfoot-Hunchback-No-lips talked to Duke Ling of Wei. Duke Ling was so delighted with him that when he saw normal people, their necks appeared thin and scraggy. Jug-Jar-Big-goiter talked to Duke Huan of Chi. Duke Huan was so delighted with him that when he saw normal people, he too thought their necks were thin and scraggy. So when goodness shines forth, the outward appearances are forgotten. We do not forget what ought to be forgotten, but forget what ought not be forgotten. This is forgetfulness indeed!

Therefore, the wise let everything pass before their minds. To them, learning is something added, conventions are like glue, morality is a bond, and skills are for trade. The wise do not make plans, so what use have they for learning? They do not make divisions, so what use have they for glue? They lack nothing, so what use have they for morality? They have nothing to sell, so what use have they for trade? Their not needing these four things is a gift from heaven. This gift is their heavenly food. Since they are fed by heaven, what use have they for people? They have the appearance of being human but not the desires of humans. They have the appearance of being human, so they associate with humans. They do not have the desires of humans, so they are not concerned with right or wrong. How infinitely small is that which makes them human! How infinitely great is that which makes them perfect in heaven!

闇□□□□无朕□□□□□□之所欲金人古□□有□
雍□□□□□□□□槌□□□之所欲金之□□□脆□□□
□□□□□□□□□□有□名人□□□□□□□□□□
此□□□之

坟聖人有□□□□□薛子□□□膠□□□□□之□□
聖人□□□□□□□□□用□□□断□用□□□□
□□□□□□□□大□常□□天□常□去□□□□
□□□金□□天□□用人有□之□□天人□□
□□□□□故□□北人天人之□□□□□□□□
□□□□□□□之□□□十□□
□□□□□□□□□天天

Hui Tsu asked Chuang Tsu, "Can a person really live without desire?"

"Yes," said Chuang Tsu.

"But," said Hui Tsu, "if a person has no desire, how can you call them human?"

Chuang Tsu said, "Tao gives them their appearance, and heaven gives them their body. Why should they not be called human?"

Hui Tsu said, "Since they are called human, how can they be without desire?"

Chuang Tsu said, "That is not what I mean by desire. When I say they have no desire, I mean that they do not disturb their inner well-being with likes and dislikes. They accept things as they are and do not try to improve upon them."

Hui Tsu said, "If one does not try to improve upon the way things are, how does one survive?"

Chuang Tsu said, "Tao gives them their appearance. Heaven gives them their body. They do not disturb their inner well-being with likes and dislikes. At present you use all your vital energy on external things and wear out your spirit. You lean against a tree and mutter, collapse upon a rotten stump and fall asleep. Your body is a gift from heaven, yet you use it to babble and jabber about 'hardness' and 'whiteness'!"[9]

莊子與惠子遊於濠梁之上莊子曰儵魚出遊從容是魚之樂也惠子曰子非魚安知魚之樂莊子曰子非我安知我不知魚之樂惠子曰我非子固不知子矣子固非魚也子之不知魚之樂全矣莊子曰請循其本子曰汝安知魚樂云者既已知吾知之而問我我知之濠上也

倚樹而吟摘橋而瞑

大宗師

CHAPTER SIX

# THE GREAT MASTER

知天之所為知人之所為者至矣知天之所為者天而生也其人之所為
以其知之所知以養其知之所不
知終其天年而不中道夭者是知之盛也雖然有
患夫知有所待而後當其所待者特未定也
庸詎知吾所謂天之非人乎所謂人之非天乎
且有真人而後有真知

Perfect is one who knows what comes from heaven and what comes from humans. Knowing what comes from heaven, we are in tune with heaven. Knowing what comes from humans, we use our knowledge of the known to develop our knowledge of the unknown and enjoy the fullness of life until our natural death. This is the perfection of knowledge.

However, there is one difficulty. Knowledge must be based upon something, but we are not certain what this may be. How, indeed, do I know that what I call heaven is not actually human, and that what I call human is not actually heaven? First, one must be true; then there can be true knowledge.

But what is a true person?

The true people of old did not mind being poor. They took no pride in their achievements. They made no plans. Thus, they could commit an error and not regret it. They could succeed without being proud. Thus, they could climb mountains without fear, enter water without getting wet, and pass through fire unscathed. This is the knowledge that leads to Tao.

The true people of old slept without dreaming and woke without anxiety. Their food was plain, and their breath was deep. For the breath of the true people rose up from their heels while the breath of common people rises from their throats. When they are overcome, their words catch in their throats like vomit. As their lusts and desires deepen, their heavenly nature grows shallow.

The true people of old knew nothing about loving life or hating death. When they were born, they felt no elation. When they entered death, there was no sorrow. Carefree they went. Carefree they came. That was all. They did not forget their beginning and did not seek their end. They accepted what they were given with delight, and when it was gone, they gave it no more thought. This is called not using the mind against Tao and not using that which is human to help heaven. Such were the true people of old.

何謂真人　古之真人　不逆寡　不雄成　不謨士　若然者　過而弗悔　當而不自得也　若然者　登高不慄　入水不濡　入火不熱　是知之能登假於道者也若此　古之真人　其寢不夢　其覺無憂　其食不甘　其息深深　真人之息以踵　眾人之息以喉　屈服者　其嗌言若哇　其耆欲深者　其天機淺　古之真人　不知說生　不知惡死　其出不訢　其入不距　翛然而往　翛然而來而已矣　不忘其所始　不求其所終　受而喜之　忘而復之　是之謂不以心捐道　不以人助天　是之謂真人

Such a people have a free mind, a calm manner, and an unfurrowed brow. They are as cool as autumn and as mild as spring. Their joy and anger flow like changing seasons. They are in harmony with all things and have no limitations. Therefore, when wise ones wage war, they can destroy a nation without losing the people's hearts. Their blessings fall upon the ten thousand things, but not because they love people.

Therefore, the people who desire to know all things are not wise. Showing partiality is not true kindness. Those who calculate their timing are not wise. Those who do not see through gain and loss are not great people. Those who seek recognition and do not follow what they know do not understand. Those who would lose their lives without being true to themselves can never be masters of people. Such men as Hu Pu Chieh, Wu Kuang, Po I, Shu Chi, Chi Tsu, Hsu Yu, Chi To, and Shen Tu Ti all lost their lives by doing the bidding of others. They tried to act in ways that were natural to others but not natural to themselves.

This was the true person of old. One who stood straight and firm and did not waver. One who was of humble mien but was not servile. One who was independent but not stubborn, open to everything yet made no boast. One who smiled as if pleased, and responded to things naturally. One whose radiance came from inner light. One who remained centered even in the company of others. One who was broad minded as if agreeing with everyone, high-minded as if beyond influence, inward minded as if wishing to withdraw from the world, and absentminded as if unaware of what to say.

The true person considered criminal law to be the body of government, ceremony its wings, knowledge a requirement of the times, and reason a guide for action. To consider law as the body, one has to be lenient in its execution. To take ceremony as the wings is to give people something to follow. To take knowledge as a requirement of the times is to do things that have to be done. To consider reason as a guide for action is to be with others on the path upward. The true person acted effortlessly, yet appeared to be trying very hard.

古之真人、其狀義而不朋、若不足而不承、與乎其觚而不堅也、張乎其虛而不華也、邴邴乎其似喜乎、崔乎其不得已乎、滀乎進我色也、與乎止我德也、厲乎其似世乎、謷乎其未可制也、連乎其似好閉也、悗乎忘其言也、以刑為體、以禮為翼、以知為時、以德為循、以刑為體者、綽乎其殺也、以禮為翼者、所以行於世也、以知為時者、不得已於事也、以德為循者、言其與有足者至於丘也、而人真以為勤行者也

What the true people like is the One; what they do not like is also the One. That which is One is One; that which is not One is also One. The true person knows the One and is of heaven. The true person knows not the One and is human. So heaven and human are not in conflict. Such is the true person. It is destiny to live and die, as certain as night and day. It is of heaven, beyond the interference of people. Such is the nature of things. If a people are willing to view heaven as their father and experience love, how much more love will they feel for what is beyond heaven! If they feel that the ruler of the kingdom is above them and are willing to die for the king, how much more will they be willing to do for the truth!

When the springs go dry and fish are left stranded on the ground, they smear each other with slime and spew spit on one another. It is better for them to be in the rivers and lakes, where they pay each other no heed. Instead of praising Yao and denouncing Chieh,[10] it would be better to pay heed to neither and lose oneself in Tao.

The great earth burdens me with a body, causes me to toil in life, eases me in old age, and rests me in death. That which makes my life good, makes my death good also.

A boat concealed in a ravine and a fishnet in a swamp appear to be safely hidden. But at midnight a strong man may put them on his back and walk off with them. Dimwits do not understand that no matter how well one hides small things in larger ones, there is always a chance of losing them. But if you hide the universe in the universe, there is no way to lose it. This is the ultimate reality.

You were born in a human form, and you find joy in it. Yet there are ten thousand other forms endlessly transforming that are equally good, and the joy in these is untold. The wise dwell among those things which can never be lost, and so they live forever. They willingly accept early death, old age, the beginning and the end, and serve as an example for everyone. How much more should we emulate the creator of the ten thousand things, on whom the great flow depends!

夫大塊載我以形，勞我以生，佚我以老，息我以死。故善吾生者，乃所以善吾死也。

夫藏舟於壑，藏山於澤，謂之固矣。然而夜半有力者負之而走，昧者不知也。藏小大有宜，猶有所遁。若夫藏天下於天下而不得所遁，是恆物之大情也。特犯人之形而猶喜之。若人之形者，萬化而未始有極也，其為樂可勝計邪！故聖人將遊於物之所不得遁而皆存。善妖善老，善始善終，人猶效之，又況萬物之所係，而一化之所待乎！

夫道、有情有信、無爲無形、可傳而不可受、可得而不可見、自本自根、未有天地、自古以固存、神鬼神帝、生天生地、在太極之先而不爲高、在六極之下而不爲深、先天地生而不爲久、長於上古而不爲老。狶韋氏得之、以挈天地、伏戲氏得之、以襲氣母、維斗得之、終古不忒、日月得之、終古不息、堪坏得之、以襲崑崙、馮夷得之、以遊大川、肩吾得之、以處大山、黃帝得之、以登雲天、顓頊得之、以處玄宮、禺強得之、立乎北極、西王母得之、坐乎少廣、莫知其始、莫知其終、彭祖得之、上及有虞、下及五伯、傅說得之、以相武丁、奄有天下、乘東維、騎箕尾、而比於列星。

Tao has reality and substance, but no action or form. It can be given but not received. It is attainable but invisible. It is its own source and its own root. It existed before heaven and earth and for all eternity. It causes spirits and gods to be divine. It begets heaven and earth. It is above the zenith and yet not high. It is below the nadir and yet not low. It was born before heaven and earth but not long ago. It was there before the oldest antiquity but is not old.

Hsi Wei attained Tao and brought heaven and earth into harmony. Fu Hsi attained it and entered into the source of vital energy. The Great Bear attained it and has never erred from its course. The sun and moon attained it and have never ceased to shine. Kan Pi attained it and entered Kunlun Mountain. Feng I attained it and wandered along the Great River. Chien Wu attained it and dwelt on Mount Tai. The Yellow Emperor attained it and soared upon the clouds to heaven. Chuan Hsu attained it and dwelt in the Dark Palace.[11] Yu Chiang attained it and went to live at the North Pole. The Queen Mother of the West attained it and took her seat on Shao Kwan Mountain. No one knows her beginning and no one knows her end. Peng Tsu attained it and lived from the time of Shun to the time of the Five Princes. Fu Yueh attained it, became Prime Minister to Wu Ting, and ruled the world. Then he mounted the eastern Milky Way, and riding on Sagittarius and Scorpio, he took his place among the constellations.

Nan Po Tsu Kuei asked Hunchback Woman, "You are old, and yet you look like a child. Why is this?"

"I have found Tao," she replied.

"Can Tao be learned?" he asked.

"No! How could it be? You are not the one to do it, anyway. Now, consider Pu Liang I. He has the talent of a wise one but not the Tao of a wise one. I have the Tao of a wise one but not the talent. I wished to teach him so that he might indeed be a wise one. Teaching the Tao of a wise one to a person who has the talent of a wise one seems to be an easy matter. But no, it took a long time to reveal it to him. After three days, he began to transcend the physical world. After his transcendence of the physical world, I kept working with him. After seven days, he began to transcend all material existence. After his transcendence of all material existence, I kept working with him. After nine days, he began to transcend all life. Having transcended all life, he began to achieve the clear vision of dawn. Having achieved the clear vision of dawn, he began to see

the One. Having seen the One, he began to transcend the distinction of past and present. Having transcended the distinction of past and present, he began to enter the land where there is no life or death, where killing does not take away life and giving birth does not add to it. He would reject nothing, welcomed all things, negated all things, and affirmed all things. This is called tranquillity in struggle, meaning perfection is the result of struggle."

Nan Po Tsu Kuei asked, "Where did you learn all this?"

She replied, "I have learned it from the son of Ink-writing, the son of Ink-writing from the grandson of Chanting-recitation, the grandson of Chanting-recitation from Clear-understanding, Clear-understanding from Quiet-affirmation, Quiet-affirmation from Immediate-experience, Immediate-experience from Dramatic-expression, Dramatic-expression from Dark-obscurity, Dark-obscurity from Mysterious-void, and Mysterious-void from Beginning-of-no-beginning."

南伯子葵問乎女偊曰子之年長矣而色若孺子何也曰吾聞道矣
南伯子葵曰道可得學邪曰惡惡可子非其人也夫卜梁倚有聖人之才
而無聖人之道我有聖人之道而無聖人之才
吾欲以教之庶幾其果為聖人乎不然以聖人之道告聖人之才亦易矣吾猶守而告之
三日而後能外天下已外天下矣吾又守之
七日而後能外物已外物矣吾又守之
九日而後能外生已外生矣而後能朝徹
朝徹而後能見獨見獨而後能無古今
無古今而後能入於不死不生殺生者不死
生生者不生其為物無不將也無不迎也
無不毀也無不成也其名為攖寧攖寧也者
攖而後成者也南伯子葵曰子獨惡乎聞之
曰聞諸副墨之子副墨之子聞諸洛誦之孫
洛誦之孫聞之瞻明瞻明聞之聶許聶許聞之需役
需役聞之於謳於謳聞之玄冥玄冥聞之參寥
參寥聞之疑始

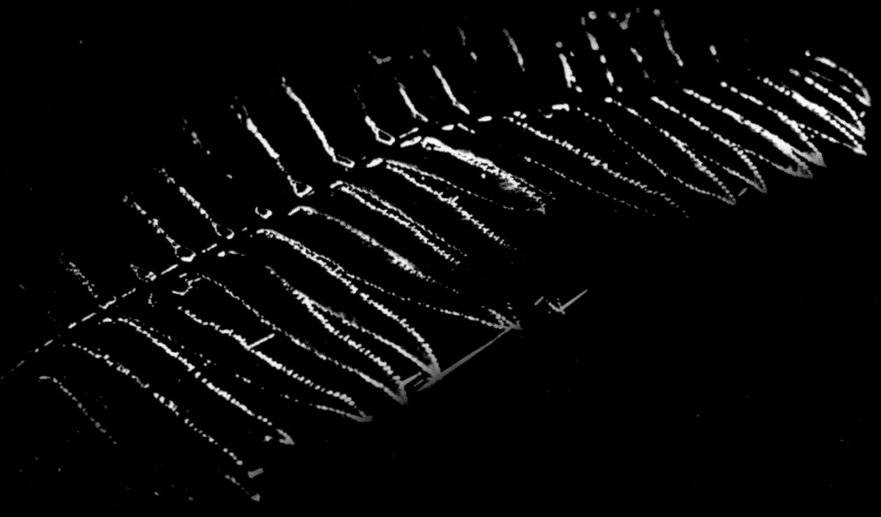

Four men, Tsu Szu, Tsu Yu, Tsu Li, and Tsu Lai, were having a discussion, saying, "Whoever believes Nothingness to be the head, Life to be the backbone, and Death to be the tail; whoever can know life, death, being, and nonbeing all as one, shall be our friend." The four looked at one another and smiled. And since they were in complete agreement, they became fast friends.

Not long after, Tsu Yu fell ill, and Tsu Szu went to see him. Tsu Yu said, "Great is the Creator that made me as deformed as this!"

His crooked spine was curled round like a hunchback; his five organs were upside down; his chin rested on his navel; his shoulders rose up above his head; his neck bone pointed to the sky. His body was sick, yet he was calm and carefree. He limped to the well and looked at his reflection and said, "Ah! The Creator has made me all crooked like this!"

"Does this upset you?" asked Tsu Szu.

"No, why should it? If my left arm became a rooster, I would use it to herald the dawn. If my right arm became a crossbow, I would shoot down a bird for roasting. If my buttocks became wheels and my spirits a horse, I would ride them. What need would I have for a wagon? For we were born because it was time, and we die in accordance with nature. If we are content with whatever happens and follow the flow, joy and sorrow cannot affect us. This is what the ancients called freedom from bondage. There are those who cannot free themselves because they are bound by material existence. But nothing can overcome heaven. That is the way it has always been. Why should I be upset?"

Shortly thereafter, Tsu Lai fell ill. He lay gasping for life while his wife and children gathered around crying. Tsu Li came to see him and said, "Shhh! Get away from him! Do not disturb the transformation!" Leaning against the door, he said to Tsu Lai, "Great is the Creator! What will the Creator use you for now? Where will the Creator send you? Will the Creator make you into a rat's gizzard or a snake's leg?"

Tsu Lai replied, "A son must go wherever his parents tell him to go! East, west, south, or north. Yin and Yang are no other than one's parents. If they brought me to the verge of death and I do not obey them, then I am only being stubborn. They are not to be blamed.

"The great earth burdens me with a body, causes me to toil in life, eases me in old age, and rests me in death. That which makes my life good makes my death good also. If a skilled smith were casting metal and the metal should leap up and say, 'Make me into a famous sword like Mo Yeh!,' the smith would surely consider it an ill omen. Now, if by chance I were being cast into a human form and I were to say, 'Make me a man! Make me a man!,' the Creator would certainly consider me an ill omen. Now, if I regard heaven and earth as a great melting pot, and creation and transformation as a master smith, then where can I be sent and not find it fitting? Thus, calmly I sleep and freshly I waken."

Tsu Sang Hu, Meng Tsu Fan, and Tsu Chin Chang were acquaintances. They said to each other, "Who can be together without togetherness and cooperate without cooperation? Who can soar up to heaven, wander through the clouds, and pass beyond the limits of space, unmindful of existence, forever and ever?" Then the three looked at one another and laughed. Having no disagreement among themselves, they became fast friends.

After some time, Tsu Sang Hu died. Before the burial, Confucius heard of his death and sent his disciple Tsu Kung to attend the mourning. Tsu Kung found that one of the friends was composing a song and the other was playing a lute. They sang together in unison, "Oh Sang Hu! Oh Sang Hu! You have gone back to your true self while we remain human. Alas! Alas!"

Tsu Kung hurried in and said, "May I ask something? Is that appropriate, singing in the presence of a corpse?"

The two looked at each other and laughed. "What does he know about ceremony?" they said.

子貢反以告孔子孔子
彼何人乎人年和修行天有而外夫形骸臨尸而歌顏色不變元以儒之
做何人乎和孔子曰彼假脩人之以忘其身况其外乎而以脩力之外乎而外乎不相及
師丘偃女徒而已孔子曰向者先生有言而適去丘未及之而逝矣丘之所左
彼此出乎而附營影城以及快執貴雖夫若此者子之誤去死生之所左
倡于里扬之託于同體忘其肝膽遺其耳目逐不相應追之逝逝忽然
忘之況而徊徊乎塵垢之外逍遙乎天下之業者彼又安能憒憒然為世俗之禮
以歡眾人之目哉孔子子又曷故而又知夫道之甚美能又憒憒然於世俗之禮
子貢曰彼然則夫子何方之依乎曰一而已矣微氏曰魚相造乎水人相造乎道相造乎水者穿也空養行
子貢曰敢問孔子曰魚相造乎水者穿池而養給相造乎道者無事而生定故曰魚相忘乎江湖人相忘乎道術
子貢曰敢問畸人曰畸人者畸於人而侔於天故曰天之小人人之君子人之君子天之小人也

Tsu Kung went back and reported to Confucius, saying, "What sort of men are they? They are badly behaved and are unconcerned with appearances. They sang in front of the corpse with no sign of emotion. I do not know how to describe them. What sort of people are they?"

Confucius said, "They travel beyond the physical world, and I travel within it. Our paths will never meet. It was stupid of me to send you to attend the funeral. They are now in the company of the Creator and are taking delight in the one breath of heaven and earth. They look upon life as a swelling tumor, a protruding goiter, and look upon death as the bursting of a boil and the draining of an abscess. How could such men discriminate between life and death? They consider the body as an accidental arrangement of different elements. They forget their livers and galls, and ignore their eyes and ears. They come and go, ending and beginning again, unmindful of any limitations. Without a care, they roam beyond the dusty world and wander freely, dwelling in nonaction. Why should they bother with the conventions of this vulgar world and make a show for the eyes and ears of the common people?"

Tsu Kung said, "Why then, Master, do you observe conventions?"

Confucius said, "I am condemned by heaven to do so. However, you and I have this in common."

Tsu Kung said, "May I ask what you mean?"

Confucius said, "Fish thrive in water; human beings thrive in Tao. Those who thrive in water dart about in the pond and find nourishment there. Those who thrive in Tao work without doing, and their nature is realized. Therefore, it is said, 'Fish need to lose themselves in rivers and lakes, and human beings need to lose themselves in the practice of Tao.'"

Tsu Kung said, "May I ask about those strange people?"

"The strange people are strange to humans but familiar to heaven. Therefore, it is said, 'The inferior person of heaven is superior among humans; the inferior person among humans is superior in heaven.'"

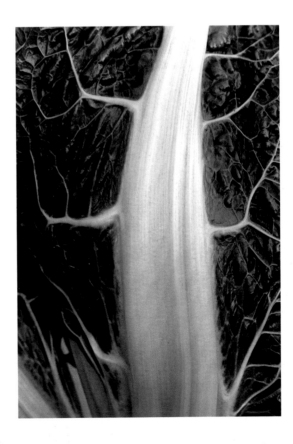

Yen Hui asked Confucius, "When Meng Sun Tsai's mother died, he cried out but did not weep. He was not sad at heart. He observed mourning without sorrow. With these three failings, he was nevertheless considered the best mourner in the state of Lu. How can one gain such a reputation on nothing? I am utterly amazed."

Confucius said, "Meng Sun has indeed mastered Tao! He has gone beyond wisdom. He has already made his life simple. Yet there are certain customs he still has to observe. Meng Sun does not know why we live and why we die. He does not know which comes first and which last. He accepts his state of being without concern for future transformation. When one is changing, how does one know that a change is taking place? When one is not changing, how does one know that a change hasn't already occurred?

"Maybe you and I are still in a dream and have not yet awakened. Moreover, Meng Sun appeared shaken, but his mind was not moved. There was a change of abode, but there was no real death. Meng Sun was the only one who was awake. He wept only when he saw the others weep; that is his true nature. Furthermore, we all talk about 'me.' How do we know that there is such a person as 'me'? You dream that you are a bird soaring up to the sky. You dream that you are a fish diving in a pool. As we speak now, we do not know whether we are awake or dreaming. Making accusations is not as good as laughing. And laughter is not as good as letting things follow their natural course. Be content with what is happening and forget about change; then you can enter into the oneness of the mystery of heaven."

顏回問仲尼曰孟孫才其母死哭泣無涕中心不慼
居喪不哀無此三者以善處喪蓋魯國
固有無其實而固有其名者乎回壹怪之
仲尼曰夫孟孫氏盡之矣進於知矣
唯簡之而不得夫已有所簡矣
孟孫氏不知所以生不知所以死
不知就先不知就後若化為物
以待其所不知之化已乎且方將化
惡知不化哉方將不化惡知已化哉
吾特與汝其夢未始覺者邪
且彼有駭形而無損心有旦宅而無情死
孟孫氏特覺人哭亦哭是自其所以乃
且也相與吾之耳矣庸詎知吾所謂吾之乎
且汝夢為鳥而厲乎天
夢為魚而沒於淵
不識今之言者其覺者乎其夢者乎
天一

Yi Erh Tsu went to see Hsu Yu. Hsu Yu asked, "What has Yao taught you?"

Yi Erh Tsu said, "Yao instructed me to practice kindness and goodness and to distinguish clearly between right and wrong."

Hsu Yu said, "Then why do you come to see me? Yao has already branded you with kindness and goodness and cut off your nose with right and wrong. How will you be able to wander on the path, freely and without a care, doing whatever you like?"

Yi Erh Tsu said, "That may be so, but I would still like to wander along the fringes if I can."

Hsu Yu said, "No, when people are blind, it is impossible for them to appreciate the beauty of face and complexion or to tell a blue sacrificial robe from a yellow one."

Yi Erh Tsu said, "Wu Chuang surrendered her beauty, Chu Liang abandoned his strength, and the Yellow Emperor discarded his knowledge. All of these were part of a process of purging and purification. How do you know that the Creator would not rid me of my brands, replace my nose, and make me fit to be your disciple?"

Hsu Yu said, "Ah! We cannot tell yet. But let me give you the general idea.

"O my master! O my master!

"The Creator has set the ten thousand things in order, yet is not attached to being good. The Creator gave life to the ten thousand generations, yet is not attached to being kind. The Creator is more ancient than the oldest antiquity, yet is not attached to being ancient. The Creator covers heaven, sustains the earth, carves and fashions all forms, yet is not attached to being skillful.

"I follow the Creator."

意而子見許由，許由曰：堯何以資汝？意而子曰：堯謂我：汝必躬服仁義而明言是非。許由曰：而奚來為軹？夫堯既已黥汝以仁義，而劓汝以是非矣，汝將何以遊夫遙蕩恣睢轉徙之塗乎？意而子曰：雖然，吾願遊於其藩。許由曰：不然。夫盲者無以與乎眉目顏色之好，瞽者無以與乎青黃黼黻之觀。意而子曰：夫無莊之失其美，據梁之失其力，黃帝之亡其知，皆在鑪捶之間耳。庸詎知夫造物者之不息我黥而補我劓，使我乘成以隨先生邪？許由曰：噫！未可知也。我為汝言其大略。吾師乎！吾師乎！齏萬物而不為義，澤及萬世而不為仁，長於上古而不為老

Yen Hui said, "I am making progress."

Confucius asked, "In what way?"

Yen Hui said, "I have given up doing good and being right."

Confucius said, "Very good, but that is not quite enough."

Another day, Yen Hui saw Confucius and said, "I am making progress."

Confucius asked, "In what way?"

Yen Hui said, "I have given up ceremony and music."

Confucius said, "Very good, but that is not quite enough."

Another day, Yen Hui saw Confucius again and said, "I am making progress."

Confucius asked, "In what way?"

Yen Hui said, "I just sit and forget."

Confucius was startled and asked, "What do you mean by sitting and forgetting?"

Yen Hui said, "I am not attached to the body, and I give up any idea of knowing. By freeing myself from the body and mind, I become one with the infinite. This is what I mean by sitting and forgetting."

Confucius said, "When there is oneness, there are no preferences. When there is change, there is no constancy. If you have really attained this, then let me become your pupil."

顏回曰回益矣
仲尼曰何謂也
曰回忘仁義矣
曰可矣猶未也
他日復見曰回益矣
曰何謂也
曰回忘禮樂矣
曰可矣猶未也
他日復見曰回益矣
曰何謂也
曰回坐忘矣
仲尼蹴然曰何謂坐忘
顏回曰墮肢體黜聰明
離形去知同於大通
此謂坐忘仲尼曰同則無好也
化則無常也而果其賢乎
丘也請從而後也

子輿與子桑友而霖雨十日子輿曰子桑殆病矣裹飯而往食之
至子桑之門則若歌若哭鼓琴曰父邪母邪天乎人乎有不任其聲而趨舉其詩焉
子輿入曰子之歌詩何故若是曰吾思夫使我至此極者而弗得也
父母豈欲吾貧哉天無私覆地無私載天地豈私貧我哉
求其為之者而不得也然而至此極者命也夫

Tsu Yu and Tsu Sang were friends. Once when it had rained for ten days, Tsu Yu said, "Tsu Sang may be having a hard time." So he packed up some food and took it to him.

Arriving at Tsu Sang's door, he heard something that was like singing or weeping, accompanied by a lute. "O Father! O Mother! Is it heaven? Or is it man?" The voice was breaking, and the words faltered.

Tsu Yu entered and said, "Why are you chanting poetry like this?"

Tsu Sang said, "I am trying to find out why I am in such a wretched state. I cannot understand it. Would my father and mother have wanted me to be so poor? Heaven provides shelter for things. Earth sustains all things. Would heaven and earth single me out to be poor? I am trying to find the cause of this but cannot see what it is. Yet here I am in my wretchedness. It must be fate."

# CHAPTER SEVEN

# THE SAGE KING

起走取向于西一跟四向帝加不至
起走起団吃罷帝大喜苦
許り吉蘭子子
蒲況子子旦而刀とう老之す
有宗氏不没秦氏
有雲子氏犹蔵仁ツ安人
かぬ久与帝の收出すむ去
泰氏女臥徐ノ徐る
女覚于于一取己ぬも二少ろ生
大を害信七地在息宗收ノすれ人

Yeh Chueh was questioning Wang Yi. Four times he asked a question and four times he received no answer. This delighted Yeh Chueh so much, he went to tell Pu Yi Tsu.

Pu Yi Tsu said, "Are you only just finding that out? Emperor Shun was no match for Emperor Fu Shi. Emperor Shun always tried to do good so that people would follow him. He was never able to distinguish between what a person is and what they are not. On the other hand, Emperor Fu Shi was calm and tranquil when asleep, and simple and direct when awake. Sometimes he would take on the spirit of a horse, and sometimes that of an ox. His wisdom could be trusted. His virtue was genuine. He was beyond distinguishing between what a person is and what they are not."

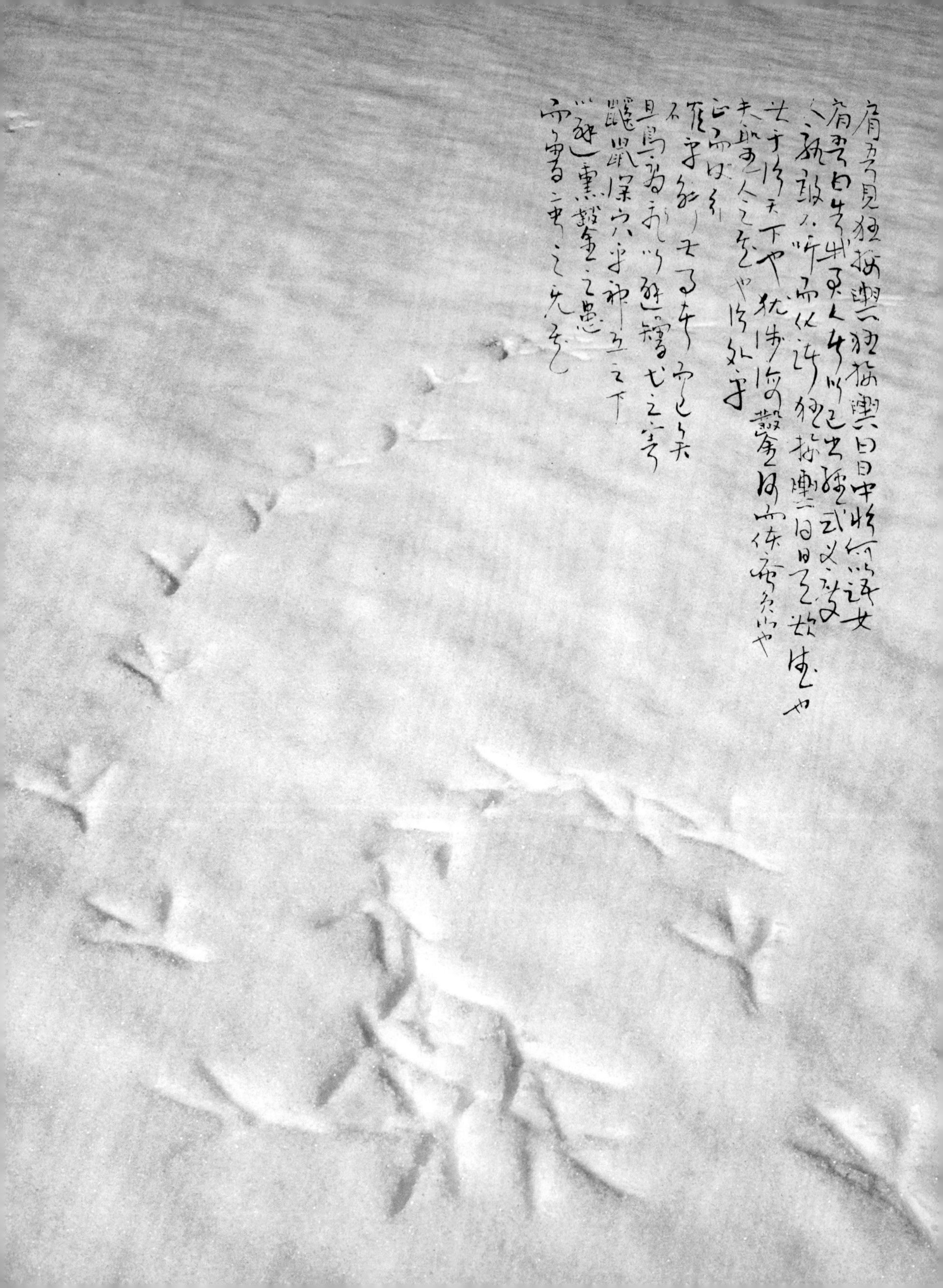

Chien Wu went to see the madman Chieh Yu. Chieh Yu said, "What did Chung Shih tell you the other day?"

Chien Wu said, "He told me that a ruler should be an example to others, establishing law and order, ceremony, and measure, so that every person is influenced and is never tempted to break the law."

Chieh Yu said, "This is subverting virtue! Trying to govern the world that way is like wading through the sea, digging a river, or making a mosquito carry a mountain on its back. When a wise one rules, are they concerned with outward appearances? When the mind is clear, then appropriate action follows. Let each person do what they can, that is all. Birds fly high in the sky so as to avoid being hit by stringed arrows. Mice make their homes deep under the sacred mound so as to avoid being smoked out or dug up. Surely people have more sense than these two creatures?"

Tien Ken was traveling on the south side of Mount Yin. When he reached the Liao River, he met a nameless wise one to whom he said, "Please tell me how to rule the world."

The nameless wise one said, "Go away, you fool! Why do you ask such an improper question? I am about to join the Creator. For enjoyment I ride on the bird of ease and emptiness, out beyond the six directions,[12] wandering in the land of nowhere and dwelling in the domain of nothingness. Why do you bother me with the problem of ruling the world?"

But Tien Ken repeated his question once more. The nameless wise one said, "Let your mind wander in the pure and simple. Be one with the infinite. Allow all things to take their course. Do not try to be clever. Then the world will be ruled!"

天根遊于殷陽，至蓼水之上，適遭無名人而問焉，曰：「請問為天下。」無名人曰：「去！汝鄙人也，何問之不豫也！予方將與造物者為人，厭則又乘夫莽眇之鳥，以出六極之外，而遊無何有之鄉，以處壙埌之野。汝又何帛以治天下感予之心為？」又復問。無名人曰：「汝遊心於淡，合氣於漠，順物自然而無容私焉，而天下治矣。」

陽の性 兒も耄耋日々人に比し絶句す泱泱果
物絶疎明・する五に動
右日らす年子此多に君子も意子や老耄白日出て卯更人や
骨稍枝條斗此少形惚本や
長史翁之る未日腹担之便物投外之物素藷
物日之午々此路え少
湯み兒熟之紙日数尚昭文之に
老明日路馬之之之路
化資万物宗氏常持功意失于而物不自己
有草大の半元
依物日喜色
立ヤ之不例
安立于元省午や

Yang Tsu Chu went to see Lao Tsu and said, "Here is a man who is sensitive, alert, strong, and decisive, with a thorough knowledge of the workings of things and untiring in his study of Tao. Could he be compared with a sage king?"

Lao Tsu said, "In comparison with the sage, such a man is like a hardworking servant, a craftsman intent upon his work, wearing out his body and confusing his mind. It is said that the reason men hunt the tiger and the leopard is the beauty of their skins. The agility of the monkey and the dog's ability to catch rats cause people to domesticate them. So how can such a man be compared with a sage king?"

Yang Tsu Chu was amazed and said, "May I ask how a sage king rules?"

Lao Tsu said, "When a sage king rules, his influence is felt everywhere but he does not seem to be doing anything. His work affects the ten thousand things, but the people do not depend upon him. No one is aware of him, but he brings happiness to every man. He stands on that which is not known and wanders in the land of nowhere."

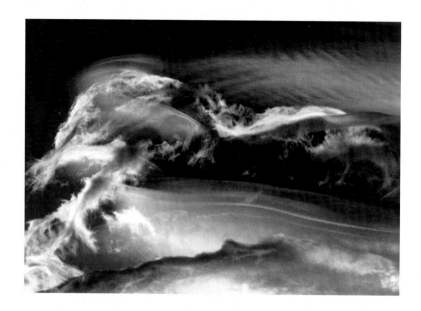

In the state of Cheng, there was a diviner named Chi Hsien. He could tell everything about birth and death, gain and loss, misfortune and happiness, and the length of a person's life, predicting the exact year, month, week, and day as though he were a god. The people of Cheng used to flee at the mere sight of him. Lieh Tsu went to see him and was fascinated. On his return, he said to Hu Tsu, "Master! I used to think that your Tao was perfect. But now I know something more perfect still."

Hu Tsu said, "I have taught you only the letter and not the spirit of Tao. Do you really think that you have mastered Tao? If there is no rooster in a flock of hens, how can they lay fertile eggs? You try to flaunt your knowledge of Tao to make people believe in it. That is why people can see right through you. Bring the diviner here and I will confront him."

The next day Lieh Tsu brought him to see Hu Tsu. As the diviner left, he remarked, "Alas! Your master is dying. He will not live another ten days. I saw something strange in him. He had the appearance of wet ashes."

His gown drenched with tears, Lieh Tsu went in and told Hu Tsu what he had heard. Hu Tsu said, "Just now I showed him the still and silent earth, the tranquil and motionless mountain. Probably he saw only that I have dammed up the springs of my vital energy. Bring him back again."

The next day the two came again to see Hu Tsu. As the diviner left, he said, "It is fortunate that your master met me. He is getting better already. He is perfectly alive. I can see that the closing up of his energy flow is only temporary."

Lieh Tsu went in and told Hu Tsu. Hu Tsu said, "Just now I showed him the heavenly void without name or substance. My vital energy comes up from my heels. Probably all he saw was my releasing the springs of this energy. Try to bring him back again."

鄭有神巫曰季咸知人之死生存亡禍福壽夭
期以歲月旬日若神鄭人見之皆棄而走列子見之而心醉
歸以告壺子曰始吾以夫子之道為至矣
則又有至焉者矣壺子曰吾與汝既其文未既其實
而固得道與眾雌而無雄而又奚卵焉
而以道與世亢必信夫故使人得而相汝嘗試與來以予示之
明日列子與之見壺子出而謂列子曰嘻子之先生死矣
弗活矣不以旬數矣吾見怪焉見濕灰焉
列子入泣涕沾襟以告壺子壺子曰鄉吾示之以地文
萌乎不震不正是殆見吾杜德機也嘗又與來
明日又與之見壺子出而謂列子曰幸矣
子之先生遇我也有瘳矣全然有生矣
吾見其杜權矣列子入以告壺子壺子曰鄉吾示之以天壤
名實不入而機發於踵是殆見吾善者機也嘗又與來

The next day the two went again to see Hu Tsu. As the diviner left, he said, "Your master is never the same. I have no way to read his face. Wait until he settles down, then I shall examine him again."

Lieh Tsu went in and told Hu Tsu. Hu Tsu said, "I have just shown him the ultimate harmony, where there is perfect balance. Probably all he saw was the depths of my vital energy in its perfection. When the waves swirl in a torrent, there are dark depths. When the water is still, there are dark depths. When the water flows, there are also dark depths. There are nine names for the dark depths. I demonstrated only three of them. Try to bring him again."

The next day the two came to see Hu Tsu again. Before they even sat down, the diviner lost his nerve and fled. "Run after him!" Hu Tsu said.

Lieh Tsu ran but could not catch up with the diviner, so he returned and said to Hu Tsu, "He has disappeared. He is gone. I could not find him."

Hu Tsu said, "I just showed him what existed before the beginning of things. Completely open and yielding, I showed myself, without a care, like grass bending before the wind and water flowing in waves. That is why he ran away."

Whereupon Lieh Tsu realized that he had not yet begun to understand. He went home, and for the next three years he did not go out. He did the cooking for his wife and fed the pigs as though they were human. He took no interest in worldly affairs. He stopped making complications and returned to simplicity. Rooted in the earth and centered in his body, amid all the confusion and distractions of life, he remained one with Tao until the end of his days.

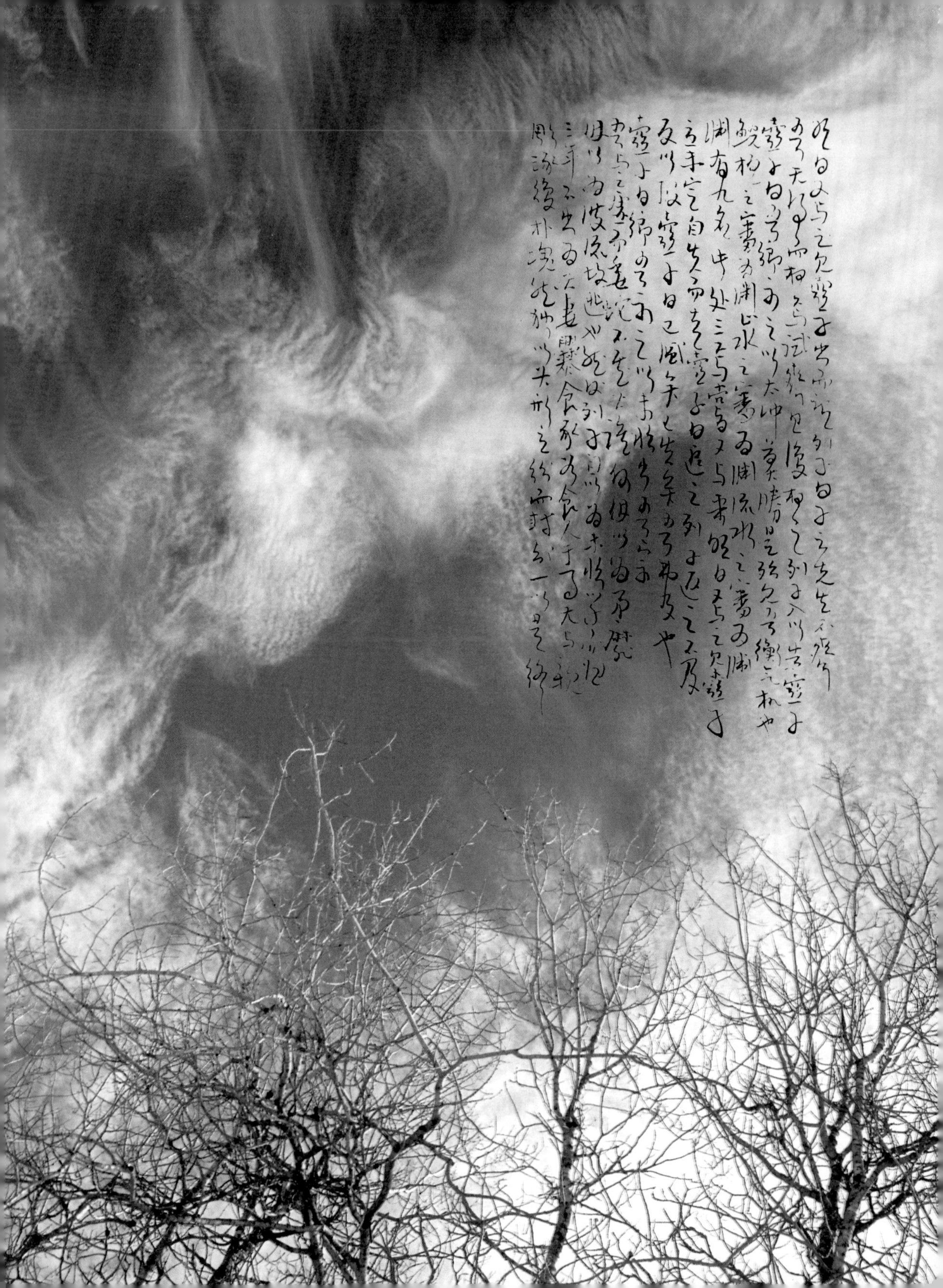

Do not seek fame. Do not make plans. Do not be absorbed by activities. Do not think that you know. Be aware of all that is and dwell in the infinite. Wander where there is no path. Be all that heaven gave you, but act as though you have received nothing. Be empty, that is all.

The mind of one who is perfect is like a mirror. It grasps nothing. It expects nothing. It reflects but does not hold. Therefore, the perfect person can act without effort.

南海之帝為儵北海之帝為忽
中央之帝為渾沌儵與忽時相與遇于渾沌之地
渾沌待之甚善儵與忽謀報渾沌之德
曰人皆有七竅以視聽食息
此獨無有嘗試鑿之日鑿一竅七日而渾沌死

The ruler of the South Sea was called Light;
the ruler of the North Sea, Darkness;
and the ruler of the Middle Kingdom, Primal Chaos.

From time to time, Light and Darkness met each other in the
kingdom of Primal Chaos, who made them welcome.

Light and Darkness wanted to repay his kindness and said,
"All people have seven openings with which they see, hear, eat,
and breathe, but Primal Chaos has none.
Let us try to give him some."

So every day they bored one hole,
and on the seventh day, Primal Chaos died.

# ENDNOTES

1. **Unlike . . . feelings.:** Lao Tsu could be a combination of several people—the Li Er who was a librarian of the National Archive, or a mythical, wise old sage of the time during the Warring States in China of the Zhou Dynasty between 1000 and 500 B.C. *Lao Tsu* (or *Lao Tzu* or *Lao Zi*) simply means the "Venerable Elder" or the "Old Child." *Lao* literally means old in age, which is honored in ancient China with assumed sagely wisdom. *Tsu* (*Tze* or *Zi*) means child, also an honorific title for an esteemed teacher or personage. As opposed to Chuang Tsu—in which *Chuang* was his family surname—*Lao* in Lao Tsu is not a surname, but rather made up to be "the wise old child." The classic *Tao Te Ching* of 81 short verses, attributed to Lao Tsu, also has many variations, and may or may not be written by him alone. The many tales of the meetings/dialogues between Lao Tsu and Confucius in Chuang Tsu's stories were clearly made-up fables to express Chuang Tsu's own philosophical musings.

2. **Chuang Tsu speaks to the skull:** one of Chuang Tsu's many imaginative ways to explore the meaning of life and death philosophically (Hamlet does the same in Shakespeare.)

3. **li:** the Chinese "mile," a measure for distance

4. **the four seas:** the Chinese expression for the "whole wide world"

5. **the hundred joints, nine openings, and six organs:** Chinese medical/acupuncture points to detail physiological parts of the human anatomy

6. **the dissension between the Confucians and the Mohists:** two philosophical/theoretical schools of the time that often had heated debates on the meanings of words and their ethical connotations

7. **the Yellow Emperor:** Also known as Huang Di, the Yellow Emperor was the earliest known leader during the Neolithic time of China around 3000 to 2500 B.C.

8. **people with piles may not be sacrificed to the River God:** Sacrificial rites required clean and healthy people for the purification. People with infirmities and unclean ailments were unfit for the rites.

9. **'hardness' and 'whiteness':** Meaning, the human body/form is heavenly endowed with yin/yang complementary integration intact; there is no use for the absolute contrast of "hard and soft" or "black and white."

10. **praising Yao and denouncing Chieh:** Yao was the prehistoric wise ruler, while Chieh was the villainous one. Chuang Tsu here is advising people to trust and follow the Tao, instead of blaming leaders/politicians for their good or bad deeds.

11. **the Dark Palace:** Chuang Tsu is referring to the "Xuan Gon," the mysterious inner sanctum within our psyche.

12. **beyond the six directions:** transcending the limits of human awareness in the six realms of Heaven, Earth, East, West, North, and South

# RESOURCES

**NEW EDITION - Lao Tsu: Tao Te Ching**, translated by Gia-fu Feng and Jane English with Toinette Lippe. Large format with over 100 new photographs and calligraphy (like this Chuang Tsu book) with Foreword by Toinette Lippe and Introduction by Jacob Needleman. Also in a small-format paperback edition with an introduction and notes by Jacob Needleman (without photographs or Chinese calligraphy). Available as an e-book. knopfdoubleday.com/imprint/vintage/

*Tao Calendar*. An annual wall calendar that uses text and calligraphy from *Tao Te Ching* and *Chuang Tsu*, with new photographs each year. Available at www.amberlotus.com.

*Still Point of the Turning World: The Life of Gia-fu Feng*. An award-winning biography by Carol Ann Wilson. Available at www.carolannwilson.info and amazon.com.

*Large art-quality prints* of the chapter spreads from both *Tao Te Ching* and *Chuang Tsu*, with calligraphy, text, and two photos, may be ordered at www.eheart.com. Prints of individual photos, with or without calligraphy, are also available.

---

**JANE ENGLISH**, whose photographs form an integral part of this book and its companion book, *Tao Te Ching*, was born in Boston in 1942. She holds a B.A. from Mount Holyoke College and received her doctorate from the University of Wisconsin in experimental high-energy particle physics in 1970. Her other works include *Different Doorway: Adventures of a Caesarean Born, Fingers Pointing to the Moon*, and *The Ceremony Cards: A Living Introduction to the Traditional Teachings of the Far North from Greenland*. Her current work may be seen at www.eheart.com.

**GIA-FU FENG** was born in 1919 in the ancient city of Suzhou. He grew up in Shanghai, where his father was one of the founders of the Bank of China. During World War II, he graduated from Peking University, part of Southwestern Associated University, a university in exile in Kunming, Free China. He came to the United States in 1947 and earned a M.A. in international banking at the Wharton School. In meeting Alan Watts in San Francisco and studying at the American Academy of Asian Studies, he found the path he had been seeking. He taught at Esalen Institute in Big Sur, California, and founded Stillpoint Foundation, a Taoist community in California then Colorado, where he lived until his death in 1985.

## Location, Date, and Medium Type of the Photographs

BW = BLACK-AND-WHITE PRINT  S = COLOR SLIDE
C = COLOR PRINT  D = DIGITAL

ii TWIGS, LOCATION FORGOTTEN, ABOUT 1973 BW

xiii CHUNGLIANG AL HUANG, BIG SUR, CA, ABOUT 1975 BW

xiv BURNT STUMP NEAR COTTONWOOD PASS, CO, 1973 BW

xvi GIA-FU FENG ON A BEACH IN MAINE, 1971 BW

2 FROSTY SUNRISE, NORTH CALAIS, VT, 2013 D

3 SEAGULL, LAKE HURON, CANADA, 1967 BW

4 SNAPPING TURTLE, IPSWICH RIVER, TOPSFIELD, MA, 1967 BW

5 EAGLE IN COTTONWOOD TREE, NEAR ALTURAS, CA, 2000 S

6 BIRD TRACKS IN SAND, DOOR COUNTY, WI, ABOUT 1965 BW

7 WIND-FORMED CLOUDS, CO, ABOUT 1973 BW

8 SUN THROUGH TREES, NORTH CALAIS, VT, 2007 D

9 WATERFALL AT THE FLUME, FRANCONIA NOTCH, NH, 2004 S

10 CIRRUS CLOUDS AND POPLAR TREES, NORTH CALAIS, VT, 2003 S

11 SUNRISE OVER MOUNT SHASTA, CA, ABOUT 1994 S

12 BIG OAK TREE IN FOG, BIG SUR, CA, 1975 BW

13 CATTLE AND MOUNTAIN, SOUTH OF PUEBLO, CO, 1972 BW

14 PEBBLES ON BEACH, LOCATION FORGOTTEN, 1992 S

15 ROUND WINDOW, SILVER PLUME, CO, 1966 BW

16 GULLS ON ROCK, BIG SUR, CA, 1984 BW

18 HORSE ON RIDGE, KLAMATH WILDLIFE REFUGE, CA, 2002 D

19 APPLE TREE, TAMWORTH, NH, 1983 BW

20 SANDPIPER ON BEACH IN MAINE, 1973 BW

21 SUNSET, BIG SUR, CA, 1983 BW

22 AT NUMBER 10 POND, NORTH CALAIS, VT, 2007 D

23 GEESE ON ICE, KLAMATH WILDLIFE REFUGE, CA, 1989 BW

24 ANT ON THISTLE, MANITOU SPRINGS, CO, 1973 S

25 CAT ON FENCE, NEAR MOUNT SHASTA, CA, 1998 C

26 RAVENS ON TREE, GOLD BEACH, OR, 2002 D

27 SUN THROUGH TREES, SANDPOINT, ID, 1985 BW

28 REFLECTION AND RIPPLES, NORTH CALAIS, VT, 2005 S

29 FALSE SOLOMON SEAL, CRAWFORE NOTCH, NH, 2013 D

30 HANGING ROCK, BIG SUR, CA, 1978 BW

31 BIRDS ON TREE, NEW MEXICO, 2000 S

32 ISLAND, NEAR SAN SEBASTIAN, SPAIN, 1983 BW

33 FEATHER, LOCATION FORGOTTEN, 1987 BW

34 RIDGES FROM MOUNT SHASTA, CA, 1999 S

35 MERGANSERS AND BRANCHES, NORTH CALAIS, VT, 2006 S

36 AZISCOOS LAKE, MAINE, 2000, S

37 BIRD TRACKS, POINT REYES, CA, ABOUT 1985 BW

38 BEEDEE FALLS, NH, 1978 BW

39 HAWK ON TREE, ROGUE RIVER VALLEY, OR, 2001 S

40 CAT AND BIRCH, JACKSON, NH, ABOUT 1984 BW

41 SUNSET, PUMICE STONE MTN., NEAR MOUNT SHASTA, CA, 1998 S

42 LIGHTNING STRIKING MOUNT SHASTA, CA, 1994 S

43 RIDGE BEFORE SUNRISE, CALAIS, VT, 2006 D

44 BIRDS ON ROCK, BIG SUR, CA, 1989 BW

45 SNOW HUMP, NEAR MOUNT SHASTA, CA, 1987 BW

46 & 47 BEACH AT SAN FRANCISCO, CA, 1988 BW

48 CIRRUS CLOUDS OVER MOUNT SHASTA, CA, 1990 BW

50 OCEAN SUNSET, BIG SUR, CA, 1975 BW

51 MALLOW FLOWER OPENING, CALAIS, VT, 2012 D

52 SEAWEED ON MAINE BEACH, 1971 BW

53 ROCK AT FOUR CORNERS, NM, ABOUT 1973 BW

54 ROCK ON SHORE OF NUMBER 10 POND, CALAIS, VT, 2006 S

55 REFLECTION OF SUN AND ROCK, GOLD BEACH, OR, 2000 S

56 GIA-FU FENG AT SAND DUNES NATIONAL PARK, CO, 1971 BW

57 SUNSET OVER PACIFIC OCEAN, BOLINAS, CA, 1976 BW

58 RUIN OF CHURCH NEAR CAMBRIDGE, ENGLAND, 1974 BW

60 CEDARS AT NUMBER 10 POND, VT, 2012 D

61 DINGHY, NOVA SCOTIA, CANADA, 1973 BW

62 HAND IN STREAM, MT. TAMALPAIS, CA, 1981 BW

63 AN ISLAND BEACH, NORTH OF VICTORIA, BC, CANADA, 1988 BW

64 FULL MOON, NORTH CALAIS, VT, 2012 D

65 RANCH NEAR ALTURAS, CA, 1997 S

66 FRIENDSHIP SLOOP AT MONHEGAN ISLAND, ME, 1975 BW

67 WATER LILY, NORTH CALAIS, VT, 2007 D

68 BEE ON HOLLYHOCK, NORTH CALAIS, VT, 2012 D

69 IRON MTN. FROM HALLS LEDGE, JACKSON, NH, 2012 D

70 NEAR TULELAKE, CA, 2002 D

71 AT SACO LAKE, CRAWFORD NOTCH, NH, 2013 D

72 SAN FRANCISCO FROM MT. TAMALPAIS, CA, 2002 S

73 ON IRON MTN., JACKSON, NH, 1993 C

74 ATTERSEE, AUSTRIA, 2012 D

75 BARN WINDOW, JACKSON, NH, 1997 BW

76 FIDDLEHEADS, JACKSON, NH, 1984 BW

77 SUN THROUGH FIRS, SANTA CRUZ MTNS., CA, 1981 BW

78 LARGE BEECH TREE, LONDON, 1976 BW

79 CEDAR TREE NEAR MOUNT SHASTA, CA, 2002 S

80 OAK TREE NEAR CHAMBORD, FRANCE, 1974 BW

81 ROBIN AND MOON, NORTH CALAIS, VT, 2013 D

82 TINY MAN 7 BIG TREES, HAMPSTEAD HEATH, LONDON, 1976 BW

83 OAK TREE IN FALL, MOUNT SHASTA, CA, 1994 S

84 OLD SILO, CALAIS, VT, 1971 BW

85 APPLE TREE, NORTH CALAIS, VT, 2012

86 & 87 FOREST ON THE BLUE RIDGE, VA, 1972

88 ELK VERTEBRAE, COLORADO, 1972 BW

90 FOOT IN GRASS, MOUNT SHASTA, CA, ABOUT 1999 BW

91 ROCK AND SUN, GOLD BEACH, OR, 2000 S

92 & 93 ELK VERTEBRAE, COLORADO, 1972 BW

94 COWPIE, BOLINAS, CA, 1976 S

95 AT MINERAL HOT SPRINGS, COLORADO, 1971 BW

96 WOOD PATTERNS, LOCATION FORGOTTEN, 1992 S

97 SMOULDERING SNAG, NEAR MOUNT SHASTA, CA, 2000 S

98 GIA-FU FENG'S HANDS, 1973 BW

99 LAVA, BIG ISLAND, HAWAII, 1988 BW

100 TAME GOOSE CHASE, CALAIS, VT, 1971 BW

101 GULL SKULL, 1968 BW

102 JACKSON FALLS IN WINTER, NH, 2010 D

103 BURNT SNAG, NEAR MOUNT SHASTA, CA, 1990 S

104 TOAD, CALAIS, VT, 2003 D

105 SAND WITH BIRD TRACKS, POINT REYES, CA, 1985 BW

106 GIA-FU FENG NAPPING, NEAR POCONO, PA, 1971 BW

107 FOOTPRINT, COLORADO RIVER, GRAND CANYON, AZ, 1973 BW

108 TREES AND REFLECTIONS, LAKE MENDOTA, MADISON, WI, 1967 BW

110 SUGAR PINE ON BLACK BUTTE, NEAR MOUNT SHASTA, CA, 2001 S

111 ICE ON A CLIFF NEAR PIKES PEAK, COLORADO, 1972 BW

112 WAVES, LOCATION AND DATE FORGOTTEN, BW

113 SOUTHERN OREGON COAST, 1999 S

114 REFLECTION, NUMBER 10 POND, CALAIS, VT, 2003 S

115 CLOUDS AND GRASS, POINT REYES STATION, CA, 1986 BW

116 BLOODROOT FLOWER, CALAIS, VT, 2003 S

117 CLOUDS AND RIDGE, NEAR MOUNT SHASTA, CA, 2002 S

118 SEAWEED, NEW HAMPSHIRE COAST, 1992 S

119 STEAMING LAVA AT OCEAN, BIG ISLAND, HAWAII, 1988 BW

120 GRASS, SOMEWHERE IN WISCONSIN, ABOUT 1965 BW

121 FALL OAK LEAVES, NEAR MOUNT SHASTA, CA, 1994 S

122 LEAF IN STREAM, NEAR MOUNT SHASTA, CA, 1996 BW

123 FOGGY FOREST, JACKSON, NH, 1998 C

124 ELM BRANCHES, MADISON, WI, ABOUT 1967 BW

125 FERN IN THE REDWOOD FOREST, CA, ABOUT 1971 BW

126 FERN, LOCATION FORGOTTEN, ABOUT 1968 BW

127 NOVEMBER TREES AND SKY, CALAIS, VT, 2007 D

128 FOREST AND MOUNTAIN NEAR KONIGSEE, BAVARIA, 2012 D

129 DEW ON MAPLE LEAF, NEW HAMPSHIRE, 1967 S

130 SQUIGGLES, NUMBER 10 POND, CALAIS, VT, 2011 D

131 FERN NEAR POINT REYES, CA, 1987 BW

132 OLD CEDAR TREE NEAR MOUNT SHASTA, CA, ABOUT 1997 S

133 CHARD LEAF, BIG SUR, CA, 1978 BW

134 BIRCH AND SUN, NORTH CALAIS, VT, 2013 D

135 IN THE PYRENEES, SPAIN, 1983 BW

136 HOLLYHOCK AND POLLEN, NORTH CALAIS, VT, 2012 D

137 FERNS AT WONALANCET FALLS, NH, 2005 S

138 LENTICULAR CLOUD FORMING OVER MOUNT SHASTA, CA, 1993 S

139 SUNSET NEAR MOUNT SHASTA, CA, 1998 S

140 BEACH PATTERNS, BIG SUR, CA, 1975 BW

141 STONE, BIG SUR, CA, 1978 BW

142 KONIGSEE, BAVARIA, GERMANY, 2012 D

144 BIRCH REFLECTION, CALAIS, VT, 2005 S

145 CAT, JACKSON, NH, 2000 S

146 CRANE TRACKS, NEAR MOUNT SHASTA, CA, 2001 S

147 BUSH AND SNOW, NEAR MOUNT SHASTA, CA, 1988 BW

148 ELM, CONWAY, NH, 1995 BW

149 ASPEN TREES, NEAR ASPEN, CO, ABOUT 1973 BW

150 MOON AND FIRS, NEAR MOUNT SHASTA, CA, 1988 BW

151 GREAT BLUE HERON, TULE LAKE, CA, 1989 BW

152 CURLY CLOUDS, NEAR MOUNT SHASTA, ABOUT 2001 S

153 MOUNT SHASTA AT SUNSET, CA, 2000 S

154 GRASS AND LOG IN A MOUNTAIN MEADOW, CA, 2002 S

155 HIGH CIRRUS CLOUDS AND POPLAR TREES, CALAIS, VT, 2003 S

156 SUMMER SOLSTICE SUNRISE OVER MOUNT SHASTA, CA, 1988 BW

157 SAW-WHET OWL, BIG SUR, CA, 1975 BW

158 CLOUD SWIRLS, NEAR MOUNT SHASTA, CA, 1992 S

159 GLACIAL ERRATIC BOULDER, TWIN MTN., NH, 2007 D

164 BERRY BUSH, JACKSON, NH, ABOUT 1998

# ABOUT THE PHOTOGRAPHS

The photographs in this book do not illustrate the text, nor does the text serve as captions for the photographs. Rather, the text and the images will take you on two parallel journeys, with occasional literal connections. In several of the chapters, I chose to limit the images to certain themes that, for me, resonated with the text in that chapter. Chapter Four, "Human Affairs," contains photographs that bear the mark of humans, while Chapter Five, being about all kinds of oddities, seemed the perfect place for my "oddball" photographs.

With the evolution of the "digital darkroom" provided by computers and software like Photoshop and InDesign, I have been able to resize Gia-fu's calligraphy and use some of my favorite photographs that did not have space for large blocks of calligraphy. I have also rearranged the columns of some of the calligraphy on full-page photos, which for the original 1974 edition were wrapped around small photos. Another advantage of the evolving digital technology is that I can now make archival inkjet prints of my photographs that equal or surpass what I used to create in the darkroom. See the Resources (p. 162) for more information.

The first version of *Chuang Tsu: Inner Chapters* that I did with Gia-fu in 1974 contained about 150 photographs. In the 1997 edition, some of these were replaced by about 70 new photographs; then almost 100 photographs (some from 1974 and some from 1997) were again replaced in the 2007 edition. For this 2014 edition, I have replaced about 30 images used in the previous three editions with photographs I made between 2007 and 2014.

In 2002 I moved back to the same small Vermont town where Gia-fu and I created our *Tao Te Ching* and where many of the photographs in the 1974 version of *Chuang Tsu: Inner Chapters* were made. I have come full circle!

— *Jane English*
Calais, Vermont, 2014

# Hay House Titles of Related Interest

*YOU CAN HEAL YOUR LIFE*, the movie, starring Louise Hay & Friends
(available as a 1-DVD program and an expanded 2-DVD set)
Watch the trailer at: www.LouiseHayMovie.com

*THE SHIFT*, the movie,
starring Dr. Wayne W. Dyer
(available as a 1-DVD program and an expanded 2-DVD set)
Watch the trailer at: www.DyerMovie.com

*CHANGE YOUR THOUGHTS—CHANGE YOUR LIFE: Living the Wisdom of the Tao*,
by Dr. Wayne W. Dyer

*LIVING THE WISDOM OF THE TAO: The Complete Tao Te Ching and Affirmations*,
by Dr. Wayne W. Dyer

*RETURNING TO THE LAKOTA WAY: Old Values to Save a Modern World*,
by Joseph M. Marshall III

*YOUR HIDDEN SYMMETRY: How Your Birth Date Reveals the Plan for Your Life*,
by Jean Haner

All of the above are available at your local bookstore,
or may be ordered by contacting Hay House (see next page).

We hope you enjoyed this Hay House book.
If you'd like to receive our online catalog featuring additional information on Hay House books and products,
or if you'd like to find out more about the Hay Foundation, please contact:

Hay House, Inc., P.O. Box 5100, Carlsbad, CA 92018-5100
(760) 431-7695 or (800) 654-5126
(760) 431-6948 (fax) or (800) 650-5115 (fax)
www.hayhouse.com® • www.hayfoundation.org

*Published and distributed in Australia by:* Hay House Australia Pty. Ltd., 18/36 Ralph St., Alexandria NSW 2015
*Phone:* 612-9669-4299 • *Fax:* 612-9669-4144 • www.hayhouse.com.au

*Published and distributed in the United Kingdom by:* Hay House UK, Ltd., Astley House, 33 Notting Hill Gate,
London W11 3JQ • *Phone:* 44-20-3675-2450 • *Fax:* 44-20-3675-2451 • www.hayhouse.co.uk

*Published and distributed in the Republic of South Africa by:* Hay House SA (Pty), Ltd., P.O. Box 990,
Witkoppen 2068 • *Phone/Fax:* 27-11-467-8904 • www.hayhouse.co.za

*Published in India by:* Hay House Publishers India, Muskaan Complex, Plot No. 3, B-2, Vasant Kunj,
New Delhi 110 070 • *Phone:* 91-11-4176-1620 • *Fax:* 91-11-4176-1630 • www.hayhouse.co.in

*Distributed in Canada by:* Raincoast Books, 2440 Viking Way, Richmond, B.C. V6V 1N2
*Phone:* 1-800-663-5714 • *Fax:* 1-800-565-3770 • www.raincoast.com

## Take Your Soul on a Vacation

Visit www.HealYourLife.com® to regroup, recharge, and reconnect with your own magnificence.
Featuring blogs, mind-body-spirit news, and life-changing wisdom from Louise Hay and friends.

Visit www.HealYourLife.com today!